THE INTERNET BOOK OF *Life*

THE INTERNET BOOK OF Life

USE THE WEB TO GROW
RICHER, SMARTER, HEALTHIER, AND HAPPIER

Irene E. McDermott

CyberAge Books
Medford, New Jersey

First printing, 2011

The Internet Book of Life: Use the Web to Grow Richer, Smarter, Healthier, and Happier

Copyright © 2011 by Irene E. McDermott

Library of Congress Cataloging-in-Publication Data

McDermott, Irene E., 1959-
 The internet book of life : use the web to grow richer, smarter, healthier, and happier /
Irene E. McDermott.
     p. cm.
 Includes index.
 ISBN 978-0-910965-89-7 (pbk.)
 1. Computer network resources--Directories. 2. Web sites--Directories. I. Title.
 ZA4201.M355 2011
 025.0422--dc22

                                                                    2011008135

Printed and bound in the United States of America

President and CEO: Thomas H. Hogan, Sr.
Editor-in-Chief and Publisher: John B. Bryans
VP Graphics and Production: M. Heide Dengler
Managing Editor: Amy M. Reeve
Project Editor: Barbara Quint
Editorial Assistant: Brandi Scardilli
Copyeditor: Dorothy Pike
Proofreader: Sheryl A. McGrotty
Indexer: Candace Hyatt
Book Designer: Kara Mia Jalkowski
Cover Designer: Danielle Nicotra

www.infotoday.com

To my son, Peter McDermott,
who helps me to write *our* book of life every day

Contents

Acknowledgments

In 2002, I had the privilege of speaking to the Library of Congress about reference resources available to librarians on the growing World Wide Web. My sister, Patricia Bowman, accompanied me and insisted that I share these helpful sites with the world. Thanks to her for planting the seed for an internet resource guide for consumers.

The brilliant Barbara Quint, who edited this book and also my monthly column "Internet Express" in *Searcher* magazine, jumped on the idea. She has urged me ever since to write this guide, which is based loosely on more than 12 years of columns. *The Internet Book of Life* is her title and would not exist without her.

I wouldn't have had time to write a book without the tremendous generosity of my city librarian, Ann Dallavalle; our boss, community services director, Lucy Garcia; and my co-workers at the Crowell Public Library in San Marino, who allowed me to take half-days off for months.

I am grateful to my sister-in-law, Judy McDermott, who read my raw chapters with her professional eye.

A special thanks to my Facebook friends, especially Mike Monroney, for giving me feedback and offering site suggestions. I also thank my special friend, Travis Deal, who supported me with love through this whole process.

I am deeply obliged to John B. Bryans, Amy Reeve, and the whole crew at Information Today, Inc. They know how to make an author look good! Thanks also to John and Tom Hogan Sr. for believing in the book and publishing it.

Finally, hats off to my son Peter, who tolerated his mom writing in the living room with all the grace that an adolescent can muster. Thanks for taking out the trash, folding the clothes, and turning down the TV. You're the best kid ever.

About the Blog

imcdermott.wordpress.com

Print abides, but the web is ever changing. So how can a print book about the web keep current? By having its own blog, of course. On *The Internet Book of Life* blog, at imcdermott.wordpress.com, I not only maintain an up-to-date listing of the links in my book. I also feature interesting, useful new ones that I come across in my work on the reference desk at the public library.

If you have questions or suggestions, please feel free to email me at imcdermott@gmail.com.

Disclaimer

Neither the publisher nor the author make any claim as to the results that may be obtained through the use of the supporting blog or of any of the internet resources it references or links to. Neither publisher nor author will be held liable for any results, or lack thereof, obtained by the use of this blog or any of its links; for any third-party charges; or for any hardware, software, or other problems that may occur as the result of using it. This blog is subject to change or discontinuation without notice at the discretion of the publisher and author.

Foreword

There's something mystical about librarians. They just seem to *know* stuff. Volumes of stuff. Acres of stuff. Informational tidbits flow from them effortlessly, like water gushing from the fountains of Rome:

Q: What's the population of Estonia?

A: About 1.34 million people in January 2011.

Q: Is Easter Island independent?

A: No, Chile annexed it in 1888.

Q: What does RBOC stand for?

A: Regional Bell Operating Company, from the AT&T break-up back in 1984.

Q: In *12 Angry Men*, how many people were on the jury with Henry Ford?

A: None. Henry Ford wasn't in the movie.

Q: I'm looking for a great pasta recipe for dinner.

A: Try peppered chicken Alfredo. But don't overcook the pasta this time.

Likewise, friends occupy a mystical space in life that's very similar to the one reserved for librarians. Friends know what you like, what you love, and even what you pretend to like just because it makes them happy. They think of you as they go through their days, watching for things that will make you smile or laugh. They listen for information you need to know and make notes about warnings that could save you from harm.

Your friends come through for you when you face problems, giving you a hand up or helping you dig out. They celebrate with you when you feel joyous and completely on top of the world, and sit quietly with you when you simply need someone there.

And the very best friends order your favorite delivery pizza for you because you had *that* kind of day—you know, the one that leaves you with the odd twitch in your right eye.

So if librarians are so special, and friends are equally special in their own way, then a friend who's also a librarian is the ultimate combination, right?

Well, yes, but there aren't enough librarians to go around for that, which is why Irene McDermott created this book just for you. Think of *The Internet Book of Life* as a completely portable, deeply insightful friend, who just happens to be a fabulously knowledge-able librarian at the same time. (Granted, this book is smaller and slightly more rectangular in form than most of your friends and many librarians, but I'm sure you can get past that in time.)

Whether you need insight, direction, caution, reflection, enter-tainment, or fact-checking assistance, *The Internet Book of Life* can help. Between these covers, Irene captures links to the best sites and sources the internet offers.

More importantly, she organizes it all to give you quick and easy (and safe!) access to what you need to know, all wrapped in the caring attention of a friend's smile, researched with the ruthless efficiency of a librarian on a mission, and delivered with the speed of a husband who just remembered his anniversary. (Trust me, I move *really* fast during moments like that.)

With this book at your side, your computer in hand, and your internet connection poised and ready, you can take on your world—or at least find the information you need in order to do it.

—John Kaufeld
Best-selling author, speaker, and all-around Chief Elf
jkaufeld@aol.com; www.johnkaufeld.com

Introduction
The Librarian's Secret

The economic climate has been so rough over the last few years that many cities have had to cut back on library service. "So what?" barked the caller to the local talk radio show. "We get everything over the internet."

What the caller did not know was that nearly one-third of the U.S. population gets access to the internet ... at the library![1]

When people think of libraries, they think of books. Yet, since the web came on the scene in about 1995, library use has increased by 50 percent. Many library users come for the computers and pick up a best seller on the way out.

So, the internet has been nothing but good for libraries. I know that I owe my career to it. I studied for my master's degree from 1993 to 1995, just as the graphical web emerged. My first job was an internship at the Getty Institute for the Arts, where I was charged with learning about the web and teaching it to the librarians there. My office that summer overlooked the Santa Monica Bay. But the stunning view of sailboats on the water might as well have been a painting. My eyes were glued to the computer screen.

The skills that I learned that summer while playing with the baby web landed me a "cybrarian" gig at the University of Southern California and, later, my current job as reference librarian and systems manager at Crowell Public Library in San Marino, California.

When my husband became ill with colon cancer in 1998, I used the web to find an experimental treatment that saved his life. Unfortunately, even the latest medical research could not save him from the glioma that took him from us in 2008. Still, we were active partners in the treatments that prolonged and enhanced the quality of his life thanks to timely information that I found on the internet.

A couple of years later, after I felt sufficiently recovered, I turned to an online dating site to find new love, a marvelous divorced dad who healed my lonesome, broken heart.

As a mom, I find the web essential for managing my household. I use it to shop, find recipes, make travel plans, bank, and even learn how to make repairs around the house. My son has become a search master while using it for school. We keep in touch with friends and relatives through social networking sites like Facebook and Twitter.

When I purchased an Android-based smart phone, I was delighted to discover the world of "apps"—little phone-based computer programs that perform specific functions. My phone came equipped with GPS (global positioning system) technology that gives it a sense of location. Apps on my phone use this information to inform me about nearby restaurants, for example, and then give me turn-by-turn directions for getting there.

Since apps act like the internet and often tie into websites, I have included a selection of them throughout the book along with tips on where to find more.

In the Old Testament of the Bible, the "Book of Life" contains the names of righteous souls. My book of life lists the names of righteous web resources: reliable, useful sites on a variety of subjects designed to help you and your family in all aspects of daily life.

Keep this book by your computer or at your smart phone charging station. Use it as a reference, dipping into sections as you need them. Some chapters—the one on divorce, for example—I hope you will never need. Still, if it comes to that, I hope that my "travel guide to the web" will prove useful.

Now you know the librarian's secret: how to easily find helpful, dependable, and even life-saving information on the internet, mostly for free, any time you need it. I can't include every useful website in this book, of course. There is an almost infinite world of information on the web, so explore, reader, explore. Still, if you can't find what you are looking for within about 20 minutes, feel free to call the expert web searchers at your local library!

Endnote

1. Samantha Becker, Michael D. Crandall, Karen E. Fisher, Bo Kinney, Carol Landry, and Anita Rocha, *Opportunity for All: How the American Public Benefits from Internet Access at U.S. Libraries* (IMLS-2010-RES-01) (Washington, D.C.: Institute of Museum and Library Services, 2010).

1

The Basics:
Quick Lookups and Computer Tips

Go ahead, ask me anything. Because that is my job at the local public library: to answer any question that is asked of me, as factually and completely as I can.

You can imagine how tough this was before the age of the internet. We librarians would flip through card catalogs or volumes of indexes, year by year, to find citations for books or magazine articles. We then followed these pointers to the shelf, where we paged through books or journals to see if they held the needed information. Bingo? We would scratch the result on a piece of paper.

We librarians keep a shelf of books near our desk labeled "Ready Reference." These are books that offer quick answers to frequently asked questions: dictionaries, maps, encyclopedias, phone books, and almanacs.

Today, the Ready Reference bookshelf gathers dust, because when someone comes into the library and asks me a question, I almost always swivel to my computer to look it up. When I find the answer, often in seconds, I send it to the laser printer and then hand the printout to my satisfied customer. Next question?

Librarians have favorite websites that we use all the time to quickly answer patron questions. First among them, of course, is Google.

There's a reason that Google became a verb: It makes the vast web usable. Here are some tips to make it work even better.

Google

www.google.com

When those clever Stanford boys, Larry Page and Sergey Brin, found a better way to trap relevant search results on the internet, the World Wide Web beat a path to their door. Now, their invention has grown so clever that it even compensates for typing errors and completes our questions, like a spouse.

Still, librarians know that Google can work even better with a couple of tweaks. My favorite is to clump a search phrase together with quotation marks. For example, sometimes I remember one line of a poem and want to know the rest of it. So I go to Google and type, *"I have slipped the surly bonds of Earth."* (I put it in quotes so that Google searches the phrase as a piece.) Sure enough, when I click the search button, up pops the poem "High Flight" by John Gillespie Magee Jr.

If you use Google but are not getting the results that you want, try using its Advanced Search page (www.google.com/advanced_search). Here you can restrict your query to specific sites (like YouTube) or leave unwanted words out of a query. For instance, if you want to know more about cats called jaguars, you can ask Google to refrain from searching for the car of the same name.

Words

Google can also work as a dictionary. When I don't know the meaning of a word, I sometimes go to Google and type *define:* and then the term. I get a list of definitions from various sources.

Here are a few specialized online dictionaries, including one from Google.

Merriam-Webster Online

www.merriam-webster.com

All of the most necessary writing and reading tools are here: your plain vanilla English dictionary, a thesaurus, a Spanish-English dictionary, and one that defines medical terms and then pronounces them aloud. I keep Merriam-Webster in all my internet shortcut lists for easy access.

Urban Dictionary

www.urbandictionary.com

Conan O'Brien recently described someone as "crunked up." Crunk? What does that mean? Search the Urban Dictionary to find the definition of slang terms. In this case, *crunk* is a combination

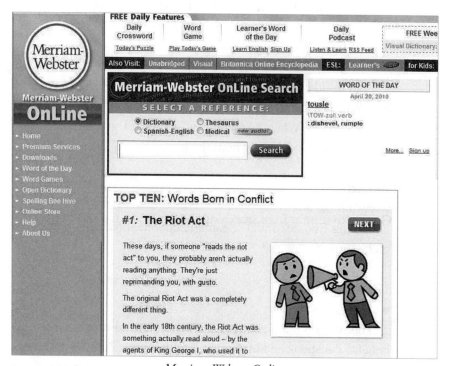

Merriam-Webster Online

of the words *crazy* and *drunk*. Be aware that this is one of the *least* vulgar definitions in the Urban Dictionary.

Google Language Tools

www.google.com/language_tools

Here's Google again, this time with tools for translating text. Need to understand a French web page? Want to know how to say something in Spanish? Just want to know what a "Buchladen" is? Google Language Tools offers a machine translation on the fly. The translated prose isn't always smooth, but it is usually clear enough to make out the meaning. It even translates Chinese!

People

Who uses telephone books anymore? If a person owns property, has a listed land line phone, or has a presence on the web, it is easy to find him or her using these free tools.

The Official WhitePages

www.whitepages.com

Find listed phone numbers for people and businesses in the U.S. The WhitePages also does reverse searches with phone numbers and addresses. When I entered my address, I got my name, my number, and a map to my house!

Infobel

www.infobel.com

Calling Europe? India? Search telephone directories across the globe through this site.

123people.com

www.123people.com

This site not only searches phone books and property records, but also Facebook and MySpace. It finds email addresses and mentions of a person's name in blogs and news stories. 123people.com can find obscure references on the web, but the correct results are often mixed with lots of false hits. I found several women with my exact name across the nation.

Ancestors

To find evidence of ancestors is to feel a deep link with your family across time. Although many genealogical databases charge for searching their records, there is much information that is available for free. Here are some starting points for building your family tree.

Social Security Death Index
ssdi.rootsweb.ancestry.com

This site finds birth and death dates for those who collected payments from Social Security and then passed on.

FamilySearch
www.familysearch.org

The Church of Jesus Christ of Latter Day Saints runs this search site that pulls biographical information from their church files as well as the Social Security Death Index.

Statue of Liberty-Ellis Island Foundation
www.ellisisland.org

Did your ancestors come to America via the Port of New York between 1892 and 1924? In return for free registration, find their entry records on this free database.

Cyndi's List of Genealogy Sites on the Internet
www.cyndislist.com

Do you want to delve deeply into your family's history? Start with Cyndi's List, a directory of links to genealogical databases. Browse her categories (everything from "England" to "Baptist") or just search her site by word. If you are unsure how to begin, start with Cyndi's "Beginners" guide (www.cyndislist.com/beginner.htm).

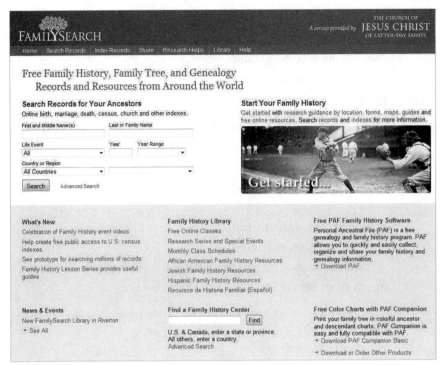

FamilySearch

Maps

Where am I? How do I get where I'm going? It's easy to find out with these tools.

Google Maps

maps.google.com

It's hard to beat Google Maps for plotting a journey. Get directions for driving, walking, biking, or even taking public transit. Google Maps shows views from the satellite and the street. It even gives information about real-time traffic problems. Download the free Google Earth program (earth.google.com) for even more dramatic mapping possibilities. Use Google Maps on your Android, BlackBerry, Nokia, or iPhone with a free app (www.google.com/mobile/maps).

Bing Maps
www.bing.com/maps

Bing, owned by Microsoft, offers driving and walking directions along with satellite and street views. Install the "3D" software to get a topographic view of your journey, similar to that in Google Earth.

Movies

Get your movie and TV trivia questions answered here!

IMDb: The Internet Movie Database
www.imdb.com

What else has that actor been in? Who directed that film? What was that funny line in that Monty Python movie? Your questions about movies, television, and actors are answered free at IMDb.

Rotten Tomatoes
www.rottentomatoes.com

Here's a movie review aggregator with the marinara metaphor. A good review gets a fresh tomato. Bad reviews equal rotten tomatoes. When a film receives more than 60 percent positive reviews, it is rated "fresh." Otherwise, it goes into the compost. "Certified Fresh" films have been positively reviewed by at least 75 percent of 40 or more critics; the wisdom of crowds implies that these movies are worth seeing. Track box office here, too, and find showtimes. Or, publish your own thoughts about movies on The Vine. This is a great all-around movie website.

Books

If you love to read, you will adore these sites designed to help you get your hands on your next good book.

Amazon.com

www.amazon.com

At the library reference desk, we use Amazon.com as a kind of *Books in Print*. It not only gives publication information, but also book reviews from reputable sources along with those from the general public. Find new releases and best sellers here, along with subject category lists (e.g., "Science" or "Crafts"). My favorite thing about Amazon is its search engine. It is very forgiving of misspellings.

WorldCat

www.worldcat.org

Why buy when you can borrow? If an item is held in any of more than 10,000 libraries around the globe, it will appear in the WorldCat online library catalog. Search for a book or a movie and then punch in your ZIP code. WorldCat will list the libraries near you that own the item and then link you through to the library catalog of your choice. Once you've pulled up your local library catalog, explore all that's available to you there, which often includes full-text magazine or newspaper articles in addition to book listings.

Use WorldCat on your mobile phone browser (www.worldcat. org/m). Android smart phone users can download the free WorldCat app from this site. iPhone owners can scan a book barcode (in the store, for example) with the 99-cent RedLaser app, which will use WorldCat data to find that same book in a nearby library.

BookFinder.com

www.bookfinder.com

Do you want to buy an old book that is no longer in print? Or perhaps you want to find the value of a book in your collection. Search the used book sellers on this site to see what your book is going for. There are textbooks for sale here, too.

Facts

"A little fact is worth a whole limbo of dreams," wrote Ralph Waldo Emerson. The web is that limbo, populated with fantasies as well as facts. Know which is which with these sites.

Snopes.com

snopes.com

Hmm, I just got an email that says that the Olive Garden restaurant chain is giving away $100 gift certificates for becoming a fan of its Facebook page. Can this be true? I'll look it up on Snopes.com. David and Barbara Mikkelson are the California couple who turned their myth-busting hobby into this trusted fact-checking site. They debunk chain letters and offer links to back up their claims. Sadly, they confirm that the Olive Garden rumor is false.

FactCheck.org

www.factcheck.org

When the political races are on, the rhetoric heats up. The Annenberg Public Policy Center of the University of Pennsylvania separates truth from fiction on this site. No computer handy? Get your facts on your web-enabled cell phone (m.factcheck.org).

PolitiFact

www.politifact.com

Did a politician make a sweeping pronouncement that sounds kind of fishy? The reporters from the *St. Petersburg Times* will research it and slap it up on their "Truth-O-Meter." See whether a statement is true, half true, or simply a "pants on fire" blatant lie.

Law

Do you need to hire professional help for a family legal matter? Here are sites that can help you to answer that question and to find an attorney, if necessary.

Nolo: Free Legal Information and Solutions

www.nolo.com/legal-encyclopedia

Need help with a common legal problem? Nolo Press publishes books that explain the law in clear, everyday language. Visit this site to find hundreds of free articles about legal situations. Topics include wills, bankruptcy, and traffic tickets.

Lawyers.com

www.lawyers.com

Find a lawyer fast at Lawyers.com. The site also offers short articles about family law.

Tax Forms

When it's that time of year again, turn to these sites to find your tax forms.

IRS

www.irs.gov

Find federal tax forms and instructions at the site of Internal Revenue Service. You may be able to file electronically for free using this site, too.

Louisiana State University Government Documents and Microforms: Tax Forms

www.lib.lsu.edu/govdocs/taxes.html

Find tax forms for your state by clicking through the directory at the bottom of the page, hosted by the libraries at Louisiana State University.

Apps

More and more of our computing is moving off of the desktop and onto the cell phone in the form of little programs called "apps." There are tens of thousands of them with more coming out all the time. Here are sites to help you decide which ones will work for you.

New York Times Gadgetwise

gadgetwise.blogs.nytimes.com/tag/apps

This online *New York Times* column reviews apps as they come out.

CNet Mobile Downloads

download.cnet.com/mobile-downloads

CNet's Download.com is a great place to find free software. It also reviews programs designed for smart phones. Select your mobile platform (iPhone, Android, etc.), and CNet will show you reviews of apps designed for your phone.

Wall Street Journal Blogs: Digits

blogs.wsj.com/digits/tag/app-watch

The *Wall Street Journal* selectively covers emerging apps.

Windows-Based Computer Tools

Linux and Apple computers are great, but most people own the cheaper (and clunkier) Windows-based computers. That is why they are such targets for hackers! Here are three free programs that PC owners can use to help a Windows-based computer run smoothly.

PC Decrapifier

www.pcdecrapifier.com

When you first buy a Windows-based computer, it often comes loaded with sample programs that you don't want. Before you start using your new PC, remove those irritating space hogs with this program, which is free for personal use.

PC Decrapifier

SUPERAntiSpyware

www.superantispyware.com/portablescanner.html

You've installed the usual anti-virus software on your PC, and yet it is acting funny. Download this program to a burnable CD or a flash drive, and run it to make sure that you don't have any rogue viruses.

CCleaner

www.piriform.com/ccleaner

Here is a program that deletes files you no longer use and makes your system run faster. It's like dental floss for your Windows-based computer.

At the Ready

I hope that these sites help you to find the information that you need quickly and easily. With the internet, help is just a click away! Still, if you can't find what you are looking for, feel free to call your local public librarian. It's our job to look things up for you!

Part One

Relationships

Amour, mes amis. Most families start with that beautiful ideal. The web has plenty of advice about love: how to find it, what to do about it, and steps to take if it doesn't work out. You may need all of these chapters as your life unfolds: how to find a date, wedding help on the web, and legal and emotional support for divorce. Many Americans go from that step right back to dating again. Here's to love!

2

Catching Love With the Net:
Dating Sites

And did you get what
you wanted from this life even so?
I did.
And what did you want?
To call myself beloved, to feel myself
beloved on the earth.

—"Late Fragment" by Raymond Carver

1988 was the year that my biological clock went "ding!" I had spent my twenties living a static single life in my tiny apartment, getting by with a leisurely part-time job, spending the evenings talking to my cat. Suddenly, it hit me: If I wanted to have a family, I would have to start dating seriously right away!

I did the math: I was 28. It would take me two to three years to find a solid prospect, followed by two years of courtship. After the wedding, we needed two childless years to establish a household. Then we could have a baby or two. According to my calculations, my family would be complete before I turned 40, with a just a bit of wiggle room.

But how to find a mate? I demanded that my girlfriends introduce me to any single men they knew. Some of the guys were nice, but all were (and most are to this day) committed bachelors.

In his book *Intimate Connections* (Signet, reissue edition, 1986), psychologist David D. Burns recommends drumming up potential matches by placing a personal ad. Burns suggests that advertisers can specify precisely what they are looking for in a date. He was amazed that his ad-placing patients could stipulate "age, intelligence, and looks, and whatever they asked for, they got!" One woman always dreamed of dating a man who owned a yacht. She "included 'must have yacht' as one of the stipulations in her ad," Burns writes. "Twenty-five men with yachts wrote to her, and she went out on moonlight cruises with eight of them."

I took Burns' advice and placed an ad in Los Angeles' alternative paper, the *LA Weekly*. I asked for responders who were literate and who had a good sense of humor. I received 42 responses to the voicemail at the newspaper, six of whom sounded highly intriguing.

In the meantime, I also answered three ads. One of these men, who described himself as "shy, bookish, and sometimes funny," called me back. He was a teacher who lived near me. We agreed to meet for coffee on a Friday afternoon. (The theory here is: I can pay for my own coffee, so there are no "financial obligations" to worry about. Also, the meeting is short—no more than 2 hours. If I don't like my blind date, I escape without wrecking my entire evening. If I do like him, we can arrange a second, longer encounter.)

"How will I recognize you?" I asked.

"I'll be reading the *New Yorker*," he said.

The *New Yorker*. This was my single household's sole subscription. I consider this weekly my mind's meal. I felt that I could not live without my *New Yorker*.

As it turns out, I felt that way about this man, too. Two years later, Phil and I married (and merged our subscriptions). Three years after that, I completed my library degree just in time to give birth to our son. Plan complete, and all from placing an ad in a newspaper.

Still, happy endings are just starting points for new journeys. Phil got sick with cancer and died in 2008. (Not part of my plan!) I cried. I cursed the fates. Still, after a year, I began to return to life. I loved being in a relationship and fancied another one. But how to begin?

I was almost 50, and it occurred to me that I was now also a single mother with a teenage son—not the most conventionally appealing date material. Still, I understand that many men around my age have endured a divorce and are back on the market. I decided to give the personals another shot, the modern way this time, via online dating sites on the web.

General Online Dating Websites

Dating is hard. We all want love; it is one of life's most fundamental quests. Back in the day, we could count on the village matchmaker to hook us up with a likely candidate. Today, we might find similar help through church or another close community.

Singles who lack a steady social group (or who wish to move outside it) must brave the choppy seas of dating strangers. The disadvantages are obvious: We become exposed to those who may not wish us well, either through physical harm, scams, or simply rejection. On the other hand, we open ourselves to the possibility of finding our heart's desire with a completely unexpected person! Sometimes it's good to shake up the gene pool.

With that in mind, I tried four of the current leading online dating websites.

Match.com

www.match.com

Match.com made it normal to look for a partner online. Started in 1995 and now owned by media conglomerate IAC/InterActive Corp, this Dallas-based subsidiary hosts a database of millions of singles from 24 countries. Match.com's slogan is "Find Love. Guaranteed." The gimmick is that users who buy a six-month subscription for about $120 and actively use the site (by writing and answering emails and keeping their profile visible) can continue their membership in Match.com for free, as long as they maintain their activity.

Users search for matches by geography or by reported characteristics, such as political belief, religion, education, and the desire for children. They may also search "Match Words," self-selected tags that members have chosen to describe themselves. Match.com serves up a "Daily 5" of singles that it thinks might fit the seeker's profile.

One caution with Match.com: Bad guys put up fake profiles with qualities and photos that seem too good to be true. They are. If the headshot looks like a stock photo, or the messenger asks to be contacted off site, do not respond. This is a scam (although those stock shot fellows look awfully appealing, especially when compared to amateur photos of real people).

Match.com has apps for iPhone, Palm, Android, and BlackBerry. Its mobile version can be reached by any web-enabled cell phone (m.match.com). Match.com, LLC, also operates Chemistry.com, which uses a matching algorithm based on the work of Dr. Helen Fisher. Chemistry.com administers a battery of psychological tests and suggests matches based on the results. It is aimed at younger, more idiosyncratic date-seekers.

eHarmony
www.eharmony.com

This private company had its start in 2000 in Pasadena, California. It was designed by Christian psychologist Dr. Neil Clark Warren to help people find their "soul mates." With that in mind, eHarmony asks each client to take an extensive personality test that rates them according to "29 Dimensions of Compatibility." The "dimensions" are grouped into four major categories: "Character and Constitution," e.g., intellect and industry; "Emotional Makeup

Match.com

and Skills," such as communication and kindness; "Personality," including sense of humor and energy; and "Family and Values," covering spirituality and feelings about children. Subscription prices range from $44 per month for three months to $290 per year. As you might expect from its origins, eHarmony is most successful for those who fit its demographic: Christian, family-oriented, and conservative.

PlentyOfFish

www.plentyoffish.com

Sign up for free to search for matches on this large database. Problem? As "POF" members pay nothing to join, they tend to be a motley bunch. The site is as unpolished as its members. For example, it distorts uploaded photos to fit into its square display slots. Even good-looking people may look unappealing when their pictures are stretched or squished. Still, there is lively activity at POF, including bulletin boards where members share questions and tales of dating frustration.

OkCupid

www.okcupid.com

Here is another free online dating site, but one with a more sophisticated design than PlentyOfFish. It features extensive psychological tests and games, which makes it a fun place to hang out as well as to find a date. OkCupid skews younger; most members are in their 20s and 30s.

Specialty Sites: Niche vs. Volume

Maybe the megasites are not for you. Perhaps you have specific characteristics that you require in a mate: political or religious beliefs, for example. Or, maybe you are turned off by the perceived demand for youth and beauty on the big sites. Face it: None of us are movie stars.

It never hurts to sign up with a "niche" site to find a date that shares your convictions. Just keep in mind that these sites tend to have a limited membership. The pickings may be thin and geographically undesirable. Still, you might find just what you are looking for!

Here is a selection of some of these specialized services.

JDate.com

www.jdate.com

Jewish singles can browse potential matches for free after a registration process that asks users to answer several crucial profile questions ("Do you keep kosher?"). Subscriptions cost between $30 and $40 per month, depending on length. The site is run by a company called Spark Networks, Inc., which also owns other specialty dating sites.

Spark Networks, Inc.

www.spark.net

JDate is Spark Networks' most famous product, but it also runs 30 other niche online dating shops. Sign up with Catholic, Christian, or LDS Mingle, SingleParents, SeniorSinglesMeet, BlackSingles, ChristianSingles, BlackChristianSingles, and even AdventistSingles.

CatholicSingles.com

www.catholicsingles.com

This straightforward site has the wrong name. It should read, "Catholics Who Don't Want to Be Single Anymore." CatholicSingles.com charges anywhere from $99 for an annual subscription to $20 for a single month. Take its "Catholic Compatibility Test," or get advice from religious leaders.

ChristianCafe.com

www.christiancafe.com

Christians from around the world, but especially in the U.S., Canada, and Australia, can search for like minds here. Prices range from $35 (U.S.) per month to about $110 per year.

Democratic Match

democraticsingles.net

"Date within your species," exhorts this progressive dating spot. Why not? It only cost $6 per month or $36 per year to join Democratic Match. If its database is sparse and likely matches live far away, so what? The site explains, "Some studies have shown that long distance relationships actually tend to be stronger and last longer than average couples."

SoulSingles.com

soulsingles.com

Professional African-American singles, meet your match here. SoulSingles.com is a subsidiary of WorldSingles.com, which also runs IranianPersonals.com, ArabLounge.com, and EligibleGreeks. com, among others.

BBPeopleMeet

www.bbpeoplemeet.com

Owned by the same parent company as Match.com, this is the leading date site for big, beautiful people (BBP). Big guys and gals can find love here!

SeniorPeopleMeet.com

www.seniorpeoplemeet.com

Until age 30, men overwhelmingly outnumber women in both placing personals and answering them. After age 40, the picture reverses completely. Older men seek younger women, while older women who have survived divorce or the death of a husband choose among an ever-shrinking pool of potential mates. This is the service for singles of both genders to find love later in life! Subscription prices range from $15 per month to $60 for six months.

Same-Sex Dating

Here are dating sites for those who fall outside of the heterosexual mainstream.

Gay.com

www.gay.com

Although some women are represented here, most of Gay.com's 4 million members are men seeking same. Become a premium member to view adult content at a weekly cost of $7 or $90 for a year. Post photos, search for matches, and email and chat with other members. Gay.com features group chat rooms, too.

Pink Sofa

www.pinksofa.com

Pink Sofa is a lesbian social networking and dating site that covers most of the world. Join for free access to site information. The ability to send messages to other members will cost you $10 to $30 per month depending on the length of the subscription that you choose.

BiCafe

www.bicafe.com

Bisexuals worldwide can meet up here. The site features chat as well as online advocacy and support groups to help boost "BiPride." Buy a three-month subscription for $19.95.

Meeting in Groups

It may be safer, faster, and personally less painful to simply meet a group of new people to see if any of them catch your fancy.

HurryDate Online

www.hurrydate.com

HurryDate offers speed dating online and in person in 70 cities in the U.S., Canada, and Britain. Speed dating involves gathering in a bar with other singles for an hour and a half. In that time, monitors move the crowd through about 25 mini-dates lasting a little over 5 minutes each. Online members can virtually recreate this experience for subscriptions ranging from $25 for one month up to $70 for a half a year. Parties add to the cost, but members can attend at discounted rates. Realize that subscriptions to the site will be automatically renewed, which means that you have to take action to stop the charges. Also, psychological studies show that participants in speed dating tend to judge others almost entirely on appearance. So look your best!

Meetup

www.meetup.com

Although not a dating site per se, Meetup offers the opportunity to meet people with whom you share an interest. Someone who shares your passion may turn into a passionate match, *non*? Chose from among almost 5,000 interest topics, attend a local meeting, and scope out the prospects.

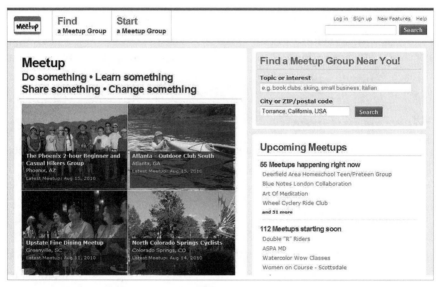

Meetup

Dating Safety

Congratulations! You've exchanged emails and phone calls, and now you've got a date! To meet safely, you know to rendezvous in a public place, keeping your address private until you get to know each other better. For even greater security, why not run a cursory background check on the web to see if there are any red flags? Who knows? You might discover something interesting about this person to chat about when you meet.

After you do your obligatory Google and Facebook searches, try these two databases for specific information.

PeopleFinders

www.peoplefinders.com

Does this person you will meet own property? In what town? With whom? Look up your date on PeopleFinders. You can infer a lot from the free information that you find there. There is a charge to reveal more specific information.

CriminalSearches.com

www.criminalsearches.com

Has your date had a run-in with the law? Find out with this free criminal database search.

CriminalSearches.com

Dating Tactics

I signed up with several dating sites and soon found profiles of fellows who seemed quite attractive! Still, although I met a series of these gentlemen, nothing panned out. Even with the wisdom of middle age and after a successful marriage, the rejection still hurt. How to cope?

David D. Burns helped me with an observation, once again from his book, *Intimate Connections*. Burns asks his readers to think about the 100 million or so people in the U.S. now successfully matched up. "Prior to their current relationship, what percentage of their previous relationships ended in rejection?" The answer? 100 percent. He concludes, "Until you meet the person you finally settle down with, all your romantic relationships will eventually break up."

So, I approached dating as a kind of scientific experiment, a numbers game in which every dismissal brought me one step closer to the relationship I craved. I tried to welcome rejection as a necessary step toward eventual success.

Sure enough, after about eight months on Match.com, I received an email from a divorced architectural designer. He looked handsome and friendly in his photo. We met outside the 1920s-era library in downtown Los Angeles. That afternoon, he wooed me with a tour and tales of the historic buildings of the city.

That did the trick. We've been dating contentedly ever since. What did I give him as a symbol of my affection when his birthday rolled around? A subscription to the *New Yorker*, of course.

3

iDo:
Weddings on the Web

Americans love to get married. We do it more than anyone else in the world (according to the United Nations, *Monthly Bulletin of Statistics*, April 2001.) Even as our society loosens the bonds of tradition, weddings still carry tremendous cultural significance.

For instance, it doesn't matter that today's women are educated and have careers. In our hearts, most of us still dream of a knight in shining armor to sweep us off our feet to live in a castle happily ever after. The wedding is the climax of this fable. It is the fulfillment of femininity, the outward sign of having attracted and captured a male of the species with only the power of our sexy adorableness.

Not only do weddings bear the burden of women's romantic fantasies, but extravagant nuptials have become a signifier of a family's wealth and stature. It's little wonder that these ceremonies support a $50-billion-a-year industry. According to the Wedding Report, an industry trade publication, the average cost of a wedding in the U.S. was just over $24,000 in 2010 (www.thewedding report.com).

29

Even when I married in the early 1990s, the average wedding came in at about $15,000. The occasion demands so many things to buy or hire: clothes, flowers, photographers, food and drink, stationery, gifts, music, a wedding and reception location, and an officiant.

My husband wanted to run away to Vegas. But I was as susceptible to society's stereotypes as any first-time bride: I craved the big white dress and the cake and the bouquet. I almost believed that my marriage would not be valid without them. Because we were both grown-ups in our early 30s, it was up to us (to *me*, really) to make this elaborate ritual happen—on an extremely tight budget.

My bible was an earlier edition of *How to Have a Big Wedding on a Small Budget: Cut Your Costs in Half* (North Light Books, 4th edition, December 2002). Author Diane Warner advocates many techniques that may seem a little cheesy, such as decorating the church community room with silk flowers and even building a false wedding cake out of Styrofoam and then passing out sheet cake to the guests.

Still, using some of Warner's tricks, we pulled off the entire affair for about one-tenth of the national norm. Unfortunately, by the time the big day rolled around, the strain of directing my own wedding almost sent me into a nervous breakdown. Oh, how I wish the web had existed when I had to plan my wedding.

Wedding "Hubs"

So much of the stuff pushed by the wedding industry seems to have little to do with the reality of starting a family with the one you love. Still, couples don't have to be at the mercy of these commercial forces. With planning, they can take charge of the chaos and make the ceremony something that truly reflects their beliefs and feelings. Web resources can help make a wedding special without breaking the bank.

As a first step in taking control of their nuptials, the newly engaged should visit one of the major wedding websites. Couples can register for free access to wedding planning software as well as web space for photos and their gift wish list. The hubs also offer great advice about marriage etiquette.

Brides.com
www.brides.com

In print, *Brides* is a 600-page glossy periodical that "opens up a world of fantasy to brides of all ages and circumstance." Its corresponding website offers registered users access to a comprehensive set of wedding planning applications, including the Custom Fit tool (www.brides.com/fashion/dresses/customfit), which lets users see how various body types would look in six popular formal dress styles. Body shapes include "hourglass," "pear," and "full figured." Don't like what you see stuffed into that teeny "mermaid" number? Visit the site's Beauty and Fitness section for tips about getting in shape in time for the big day.

The Knot
www.theknot.com

If you're tying it, you'll be buying it here on The Knot. This site provides comprehensive wedding "content," that is, information about all aspects of wedding planning. Avoid *faux pas* with advice about how to pop the question or where to seat your father-in-law's first two wives. Research ethnic and religious wedding traditions, too. The Knot lists local wedding services and offers a wedding budgeter and checklist. This is also a great place to order wedding favors. Download the free wedding planning app for iPhone: Wedding 911 (itunes.apple.com/us/app/wedding-911-by-the-knot/id32 1839274?mt=8).

The Knot

Martha Stewart: Weddings

www.marthastewartweddings.com

Miz Martha has got weddings covered. She gives advice on wedding planning, etiquette, cakes, bouquets, dresses, beauty, and gifts. Whatever she recommends is in the best of taste. Now all we have to do is follow her advice.

About.com: Weddings

weddings.about.com

Wedding planner Nina Callaway creates the About.com guide to weddings. Start with her wedding checklist that guides couples through the months before the wedding. Read her articles about creating a meaningful ceremony with particular wedding vows, music, and perhaps a unity candle.

New York **Weddings**

nymag.com/weddings

How are they hitching up in the Big Apple? Find out in *New York Magazine*'s wedding guide. Brides will find big city bargains and fashion advice. There are plenty of tips for the groom here, too.

Here Comes the Guide

www.herecomestheguide.com

Getting married in California? Here is your resource for locations, wedding fairs, the dress, the ring, and services. There are links here to wedding venues in Chicago and Washington, D.C., too.

MomentVille

www.momentville.com

You will find wedding planning advice here, but the strength of this site is its free wedding webpage application. Let MomentVille guide you through the creation of a handsome personal website that will share your love story with the family and friends who will gather to wish you well at your wedding.

Offbeat Bride

offbeatbride.com

Not all brides fall completely for our culture's fairy-tale script. Some rebel against the machinations of the wedding industry. They are in love, and they want to get married—but they want to do it their way. Seattle-based Ariel Meadow Stallings, author of *Offbeat Bride: Taffeta-Free Alternatives for Independent Brides* (Seal Press, 2007), offers advice and shares stories of weddings that ran against tradition.

Bridal Shows

Bridal shows and expos are a great way to find local services all gathered in one place. Watch a fashion show and meet with local photographers, caterers, and wedding bands.

WedAlert.com: Bridal Shows and Expos
www.wedalert.com/bridal_show
   Search by state and county to find a bridal show in your area.

Bridal Show Producers International
www.bspishows.com
   Prospective brides in the U.K., Canada, Ireland, the U.S., and Portugal can find upcoming bridal fairs here.

The Dress

Thank goodness I grew up sewing. When I married, I knew that I could put my experience to its highest purpose by making my own wedding gown. Back then, I wanted a dress just like Princess Diana's: white, frilly, and as pouffy as I could make it. I traveled to the garment district in downtown L.A. to get a bargain price on 11 yards of ecru moiré taffeta, which was enough to cover a couch—or my hoopskirt petticoat.

It took me three months to make it, but my giant gown, with grosgrain rosettes at the neckline, cost only $100. I borrowed the petticoat.

Today's bridal fashion seems modeled after the stunning, glamorous sheaths worn on the red carpet at the Oscars. The look is luxurious and sleekly royal, as befits a princess on her wedding day. At retail, the dress will set you back anywhere from $400 to more than $14,000.

You may find a good deal on a dress at an outlet. Still, know your stuff before you go shopping. Denise Fields puts it this way in her book *Bridal Gown Guide: Discover the Dress of Your Dreams at a Price You Can Afford* (Windsor Peak Press, 3rd revised edition, 1998): "The only way to educate yourself about a good quality gown is to try one on—and most expensive gowns have a certain fit and finish that you only see at that price level. ... By trying on a few expensive dresses, you'll know what's a good deal and what isn't."

Brides.com: Dresses & Style Galleries

www.brides.com/wedding-dresses-style/galleries-dresses-style

What are the latest fashions in wedding gowns? Visit Brides.com to see a gallery of current wedding dress styles.

David's Bridal

www.davidsbridal.com

Pennsylvania-based David's Bridal is a chain of nearly 300 bridal salons. It offers good value and selection in bridal gowns and other formal wear for women.

Net-a-Porter.com: The Wedding Boutique

www.net-a-porter.com/wedding

Got about ten grand to drop on a dress that you will wear once? Drop in to Net-a-Porter.com. Although you will probably not actually buy anything at this designer fashion retail site, it's a great place to get ideas for your dream gown.

Net-a-Porter.com: The Wedding Boutique

House of Brides

www.houseofbrides.com

Can you buy a wedding dress online? Sure, and you might even save some money. House of Brides claims to discount its dresses 30–40 percent compared to bridal salons. It even sells maternity bridal gowns!

BridalGown.com

www.windsorpeak.com/bridalgown

Consumer advocates Denise and Alan Fields reveal the secrets of buying the finest gowns for the lowest prices.

Ethnic Weddings

The marriage ceremony can be a time to acknowledge one's heritage. And a taste of the old country can make for a darn good party.

WeddingDetails.com: Mexican Wedding Traditions

www.weddingdetails.com/lore/mexican.cfm

Enjoy mariachi music and traditional foods from south of the border when you plan your Mexican wedding.

Chinese Weddings by The Knot

www.chineseweddingsbytheknot.com

Explore Chinese wedding traditions, attire, and etiquette.

Chinese Historical and Cultural Project:
Chinese Wedding Traditions

www.chcp.org/wedding.html

The Chinese Historical and Cultural Project, a nonprofit organization to promote and preserve Chinese-American and Chinese history and culture, offers this guide to Chinese wedding traditions.

WeddingDetails.com: African Wedding Traditions and Culture
www.weddingdetails.com/lore/african.cfm

Those who want their ceremony to reflect their African roots can explore native traditions here.

VIBRIDE
www.vibride.com

The African-American wedding tradition of jumping the broom originated during slavery times. Here you can purchase African-American wedding favors, including ceremonial jumping brooms.

Ohr Somayach International: Marriage
ohr.edu/yhiy/article.php/1087

Rabbi Mordechai Becher of Ohr Somayach International describes the Jewish wedding ceremony and explains the traditions behind it.

Bliss Weddings: Love and Marriage—Hindu Style
www.blissweddings.com/articles/art058.asp

Read Sarah Hartmann's article about wedding traditions of India.

The Wedding Cake and Flowers

To save on marriage costs, ask your friends or family make your cake and arrange your flowers.

Peggy Weaver's Baking Corner: Fondant Icing
whatscookingamerica.net/PegW/Fondant.htm

The coating that gives wedding cakes that "Martha Stewart" smoothness is called fondant. Here is a recipe for making and draping the cake of your dreams.

Cake Decorating: Fun With Fondant

www.youtube.com/watch?v=IsrgS9eB1bE

Spend four-and-a-half minutes watching Robin Hassett of the Dessert Tray prepare and coat a cake with smooth, pink fondant.

Epicurious: Weddings

www.epicurious.com/articlesguides/holidays/weddings

Get "nuptial nibble" recipes and ideas from *Bon Appetit* magazine. There is a wonderful wedding cake recipe.

Howdini: How to Make a Hand-Tied Bouquet

www.howdini.com/howdini-video-6672795.html

Watch interior designer Rebecca Cole make a professional-looking hand-tied bouquet. Cole makes it look so easy that professional wedding florists should be worried.

Michaels: Wedding

www.michaels.com/wedding

Let Michaels, the arts and crafts store, show you how to make wedding bouquets, boutonnieres, and centerpieces. There is also a tutorial on making a wedding veil. Think of the fun you'll have (and the money that you'll save) making your own wedding accessories.

Invitations and Stationery

Not since graduation have we had a reason to send out engraved announcements. Here's some help to do it without breaking the bank.

MyGatsby.com

www.mygatsby.com

Configure elegant wedding invitations online for less!

EverAfter-Bridal.com: Affordable Wedding Invitations

www.everafter-bridal.com

Order online to save 20 percent on traditional wedding invitations.

Twisted Limb Paperworks

www.twistedlimbpaper.com

How about some organic, handmade invitations? Order them from Indiana's Twisted Limb, where the work is 100 percent carbon neutral.

VerseIt.com

www.verseit.com

Here's a site to help you say it right on your invitations. It even offers a printable envelope-addressing guide.

Pictures and Music

Costs for wedding music and photography can vary widely. For example, a couple can expect to spend up to $4,000 for a fully documented, professionally photographed wedding. On the other hand, they could simply ask their guests to share their digital shots and pool them in an online slideshow for all to enjoy. Here's how to find ideas for nuptial music and movies.

WEVA International: Member Links

www.weva.com/resources.php?action=resources1

Hire a professional to create a film of your wedding. Search by state to find nearby members of Wedding and Event Videographers Association International.

WedAlert.com: Wedding Songs

www.wedalert.com/songs

Whether played by a string quartet or just popped into a CD player, music can enhance the beauty and joy of a wedding. Visit WedAlert.com to browse a list of wedding song titles. Click to listen to sound clips of popular wedding songs. The sampler will help you decide what music to play.

WedAlert.com: Wedding Songs

For Bridesmaids and What's-His-Name

These sites offer some support for the wedding's supporting cast.

BridesmaidAid.com

www.bridesmaidaid.com

Penelope the Perpetual Bridesmaid shows us how to prepare for the biggest day in *her* life. Penelope even offers suggestions about what to do with the ugly bridesmaid dress after the wedding: Make sofa cushions, throw a party and invite your girlfriends to wear their worst bridesmaid dresses, or donate the thing to a charity such as the Glass Slipper Project (www.glassslipperproject.org). This is a funny site, but it has some useful tips.

GroomsOnline

www.groomsonline.com

So far, the show has belonged all to the bride. This site prepares men for their wedding day. The best man will also find advice as to his duties, speeches, and the bachelor party.

So Elope, Already!

This wedding thing is overwhelming and seems only tangentially connected to the act of starting a new family. And, frankly, if one is marrying for the second or third time, the big dress and the huge reception seem ostentatious and slightly silly.

The answer may lie in running away to get married. Think of it: no reception planning, no family drama. It's just you, your love, and the officiant.

But wait! What if you want to bring along your friends and family? Then your romantic dash to marry officially becomes a "destination wedding." The Knot, a commercial wedding portal mentioned earlier, recommends that couples planning a wedding of any size in a foreign country hire a wedding planner. This professional can help with the vendors and caterers and ... Whoa! That sounds a lot like the same hassle we were trying to escape!

Whether you plan a sneaky elopement or a grand family reunion trip, "honeymoon-happy resorts and cruise lines around the world have made it easier and more appealing to wed on-site," according to The Knot. "Tourist boards are jumping on the bandwagon, with brochures listing ceremony sites and local wedding vendors in their area. Even governments are working to ease restrictions and attract to-be-weds."

The Knot: Hawaii Wedding Resources

wedding.theknot.com/local-wedding-vendors/
hawaii-weddings. aspx

In 1988, my sister and her fiancé got on a plane, flew to Hawaii, and exchanged vows before a lone preacher on a beach. This was the third marriage for my brother-in-law, so a "destination wedding" seemed entirely appropriate. Sound good? Visit this Hawaiian Wedding Planner to find wedding resources in the Aloha State.

The Knot also offers a directory of destination wedding planners and travel agents, international marriage certificate requirements (including those on cruise ships), and a directory of wedding resorts, domestic and foreign (wedding.theknot.com/wedding-planning/destination-weddings/articles/top-destination-wedding-planners-and-travel-agents.aspx).

Destination Weddings

www.destinationweddings.com

In return for a $50 commitment fee, register with this wedding packager/travel agency to start planning an elopement for two or a traveling tie-the-knot for 200.

Insider Viewpoint of Las Vegas: Marriage Rules of Nevada

www.insidervlv.com/marriage.html

Or maybe you just wanna go to Vegas. Insider Viewpoint of Las Vegas serves up the rules and offers links to 15 wedding chapels.

Wedding Apps

Will a tiny program running on an iPhone replace the wedding planning profession? Try these wedding planning apps to find out!

iTunes: Wedding Bridal Binder

itunes.apple.com/us/app/wedding-bridal-binder/
id351656683?mt=8

Reviewers call this $7 app "the best of its kind," with a "super detailed" checklist, budgeting software, sample vendor questions, and a way to capture notes.

iTunes: Bride Guide
itunes.apple.com/us/app/bride-guide/id319606045?mt=8

This $5 iPhone app has it all: a wedding countdown, a suggested budget, and most importantly, advice from experienced planners.

We've Only Just Begun

It seems to me that if you can plan a wedding together, you've got a pretty good foundation for a lifetime of love and cooperation. To that, I can only say, congratulations! Mazel tov!

4

UnDo:
Web Help for Divorce

We lov'd, and we lov'd, as long as we could,
Till our love was lov'd out in us both:
But our marriage is dead, when the pleasure is fled:
'Twas pleasure first made it an oath.

—John Dryden

Sandra Tsing Loh gave me a shock. The witty commentator delighted her Los Angeles-area audience for years on local public radio with tales of her family: two little girls and her talented musician husband. Suddenly, she dropped the bomb: In an article in *The Atlantic* (May 22, 2009), Tsing Loh announced that she was getting a divorce. She had had an affair, and that opened her eyes to the soul-killing banality of her marriage. So, in her words, she "called the whole thing off."

Needless to say, I can't listen to her commentaries with the same lighthearted empathy as before. Tsing Loh's whole shtick was based on her sympathetic struggles as a smart, committed mom nurturing her family. It is distasteful when a married person, out of boredom, ditches his or her spouse and kids for someone else. In the case of Tsing Loh, her divorce not only destroyed her family, but her brand.

Still, a waning of passion isn't the only reason that couples split. As the site TeensHealth (kidshealth.org/teen/your_mind/families/divorce.html) gently explains, "Usually divorce happens when couples feel they can no longer live together due to fighting and anger." Also, "sometimes it is due to a serious problem like drinking, abuse, or gambling."

Indeed, the chance of marriage failure overall is about 45 percent, according to David Popenoe, professor of sociology emeritus at Rutgers University. First marriages fare better, as do those between people who are from intact families, who are both college-educated, and who share religion.

Still, divorce is common and ranks as one of the most stressful events one can endure, apart from the death of a spouse. (Although the death of my husband was anguishing, our separation was involuntary. Divorce always involves a choice, and this can be the source of immense and enduring bitterness.) Also, divorce often destroys not only the family but its finances.

Can the web offer some relief for the pain, stress, and even expense of divorce? To answer the question, I turned to John Castellano, a divorce attorney with Ross and Parvex LLP in Oxnard, California. Most of the references that he offered are California-centric, as divorce law is state-specific. Still, most states should have resources that parallel California's. I provide entry points for these later in this chapter.

The Legal Process of Divorce

The first thing Castellano emphasized is that most couples should seek professional help to prosecute a divorce. "The court process is not set up for people who don't know what they are doing. Einstein would run into problems with the system the way it is set up now."

Castellano outlined the standard divorce process. "It's good to think of it as a timeline," he said. The process begins when the initial pleadings are filed with the court. "This starts the clock ticking." In California, at least 6 months must pass before the final judgment, which officially dissolves the marriage, is signed.

In California, there are three ways to approach divorce. The first, and most common, is the "litigated approach." In this method, the parties operate as antagonists, and both sides hire attorneys. As the divorce process unfolds, the court may make temporary judgments to resolve custody and support issues. The parties will be compelled to disclose their financial holdings in a process called discovery. If the couple can't settle their property distribution or custody disputes, the case goes to trial.

The litigated approach forces the parties into adversarial positions. Two other divorce choices encourage compromise and settlement. Mediation is the first alternative to litigation. In this scenario, the divorcing couple hires a mediator, who is often a therapist. The mediator works to get the parties to come to settlement. The parties may also hire their own lawyers to help them make decisions in their own best interests.

"This agreement-based approach often influences the outcome of the negotiation to reach a settlement," notes Castellano. "It's a psychological thing. We can often at least reach a partial judgment through mediation, filtering out issues that can be resolved. In this way, we don't create disputes that don't otherwise exist."

Here is one site that deals with mediation.

Dishon & Block: What Is Divorce Mediation?
www.cadivorce.com/content.aspx?id=600

Aaron Dishon of Dishon & Block, APC, based in Orange County, outlines the basics of divorce mediation in California.

A final approach to dissolving marriage in California is called collaborative divorce. In this procedure, each party enters into a "disqualification agreement," in which they promise full disclosure and pledge that, if they can't settle the case, they will begin again with completely new lawyers at considerable expense. Neutral professionals such as therapists, child specialists, and forensic accountants may be called in to ensure that the collaborative divorce is fair to everyone involved.

"Collaborative divorce is a hard sell, particularly for low-income clients who don't want to pay for a team of professionals," Castellano notes. "What they don't understand is that they may well end up paying for a team anyway, but not necessarily neutral and committed to settlement. The model does work!" he says. "The more invested clients get in the process, the more momentum they have to settle."

The following site provides information on collaborative divorce.

California Divorce Blawg: Collaborative Divorce

californiadivorce.blogs.com/blog/2008/12/collaborative-divorce.html

San Francisco-area family law attorney John Harding provides an overview of the California collaborative divorce procedure. Harding describes the advantages of the approach but also shows how it may not work in every situation. "If there is domestic abuse, drug or alcohol addiction, serious mental illness, or an intention to hurt the other party emotionally or financially, traditional litigation may be more appropriate," he writes.

Help for Low-Income Divorces

Laypeople who represent themselves in court are said to operate *in propria persona*, or *pro per*, for short. "But be aware that, as a *pro per*, you could accidentally make expensive mistakes. And if your spouse has an attorney, it may be even more difficult for you to effectively represent yourself," warns the State Bar of California.

How can a couple that doesn't have enough money to hire attorneys get divorced? "In California, they should go to the courthouse to consult with a family law facilitator," advises Castellano. Other states should also have low- or no-cost options for legal assistance in filing for divorce.

California Courts: Family Law Facilitator in Your County
www.courtinfo.ca.gov/selfhelp/lowcost/flf.htm

Californians can use this site to find a family law facilitator who can help them file for divorce without an attorney.

Harriet Buhai Center for Family Law
www.hbcfl.org

This nonprofit Los Angeles organization aspires "to create a community where poverty is not a barrier to those who seek to resolve critical family law matters." As Castellano exclaims, "This family law facilitator practice is amazing. It is set up like a regular law firm. It's really efficient!" Organizations such as these offer low-cost services to the *pro per* who needs to get all his or her divorce papers filed properly with the court.

Levitt and Quinn Family Law Center
www.levitt-quinn.org

Levitt & Quinn Family Law Center is another charitable organization in Los Angeles that helps poor California families with matters of family law, particularly divorce.

California Courts: The Judicial Branch of California
www.courtinfo.ca.gov

California residents can use this site to find free fill-in-the-blank legal forms as well as legal self-help advice.

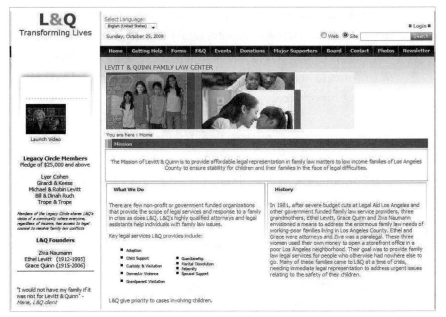

Levitt and Quinn Family Law Center

Divorce Outside California

Castellano says that he uses mainly proprietary software in his work as a family law attorney. But he did recommend several free legal websites that his clients might use to help with their cases.

National Center for State Courts

www.ncsc.org

This site features links to state courts as well as federal and tribal courts (www.ncsconline.org/D_KIS/CourtWebSites/Fed Tribal.html). Its Family InfoCenter (www.ncsconline.org/wc/Cour Topics/ResourceCenter.asp?id=10) links to articles about legal trends in marriage, divorce, and other aspects of family law. Castellano notes that information about family law facilitators can often be found on the website of one's local court.

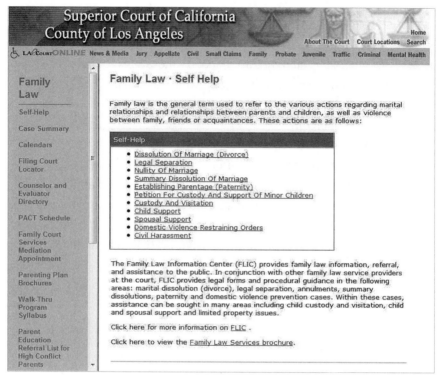

California Courts: The Judicial Branch of California

SupportGuidelines.com

www.supportguidelines.com/links.html

Virginia family law attorney Laura W. Morgan maintains this directory of links to the formulas that each state uses to determine child support payments.

Cornell University Law School: Divorce Laws

topics.law.cornell.edu/wex/table_divorce

The Cornell Legal Information Institute (LII) hosts this directory of links to the actual divorce laws in all 50 states, the District of Columbia, and Puerto Rico, as well as links to summaries of the laws. Click on "Find a Lawyer" to use LII's lawyer search service.

General Divorce Help and Advice

Dealing with the law is just one aspect of divorce. In addition to the sites suggested by Castellano, try these sites for help with emotional and financial issues along with legal tips.

Divorce360.com

www.divorce360.com

This online magazine offers advice from therapists, accountants, and lawyers to help people with the many emotional, legal, and financial issues that arise from divorce. For those just entering into the process, there is a checklist for making the decision to divorce and a section entitled "Divorce 101" that includes "What Does Divorce Cost?" This is an authoritative and professional resource, although there are lots of links to outside services. Find state-by-state divorce laws here, too.

DivorceNet.com

www.divorcenet.com

Find professionals by state to assist you with all aspects of divorce. There are also state-specific articles here, usually written by lawyers.

Divorceinfo.com

www.divorceinfo.com

Lee Borden, a Tallahassee family law attorney and subsistence farmer, does his best to ease the pain of divorce with information, including alternatives to actual divorce. Borden offers loads of links as well as an annotated bibliography of divorce books.

Military Divorce Online

www.militarydivorceonline.com

Dallas family law attorney John H. Carney offers information about the special circumstance of divorce for members of the Armed Forces. For example, military personnel may be stationed in a different state or country from their spouses. That poses problems about the jurisdiction for the divorce.

Get Legal: Family Law and Divorce

public.getlegal.com/legal-info-center/family-law-divorce

Use this Webby Award-winning site to find family law attorneys across the country.

Advice for Men, Women, and Children

As the family is dissolved, everyone involved could use some emotional support.

iVillage: Divorce and Stepfamilies

www.ivillage.com/divorce-stepfamilies/6-s-124602

iVillage hosts this collection of articles aimed at women about how to deal with the various aspects of divorce. How will it affect the kids, for example? Or one's Social Security? These thoughtful pieces help a gal think it through.

MenAlive! Male Menopause

www.menalive.com

Sometimes, men in their 40s and 50s suffer a midlife crisis that causes them to blame all of their frustrations on their wives. Therapist and author Jed Diamond gives counsel to men suffering from this "Irritable Male Syndrome" as well as to the women who love them.

TeensHealth: Dealing With Divorce

kidshealth.org/teen/your_mind/families/divorce.html

Nemours Foundation offers comfort and advice to kids whose parents are splitting up.

PsyBlog: Parental Relationships After Divorce
www.spring.org.uk/2007/04/parental-relationships-after-
divorce.php

This article on PsyBlog reviews the work of Constance Ahrons, author of *The Good Divorce* (HarperCollins, 1994). Her main thesis is that both parents will remain in a child's life, even if they split. In the best case, they form a "binuclear family, a new family system orbiting around two centers: some stable, others less so."

Help for Victims of Domestic Violence

Many divorces stem from disaffection or wandering attention. But sometimes, when a man physically hurts his wife or threatens her life, the woman needs legal help beyond just dividing community property. And, of course, men can suffer abuse, too. Battered partners may need protective orders and may even need to move away to stay safe. Here is advice for victims of domestic violence.

WomensLaw.org
www.womenslaw.org

This award-winning site tells women across the nation the legal steps they must take to separate themselves from their abusers. Women will also find tips on safety at court (e.g., enter from a side door), leaving the abuser (e.g., go to a friend's house and then leave the area), and even advice about locking up the abuser's guns and knives.

ACOG: Help! ¡Ayuda!
www.acog.org/departments/dept_notice.cfm?recno=17&
bulletin=1474

The American Congress of Obstetricians and Gynecologists (ACOG) offers help in English and Spanish for women suffering from abuse. Users can complete a simple questionnaire to see if they should be concerned about their relationship. Then, they can read tips on readying themselves to leave an abuser. The national

WomensLaw.org

toll-free abuse hotline numbers are listed in red at the head of the escape advice pages.

National Network to End Domestic Violence: Get Help
www.nnedv.org/component/content/article/162.html

NNEDV lists the national hotline numbers and offers tips for safe communication. It urges victims of spousal abuse to practice computer safety by viewing domestic violence assistance sites at their local library instead of on the home computer. NNEDV also links to state coalitions against domestic violence (www.nnedv. org/resources/coalitions.html).

MenWeb: Domestic Violence

www.batteredmen.com

Although this site, handcrafted by James R. Bracewell, has not been updated since 2008, it remains the most complete directory of resources for abused men. Find stories from men and the women who abuse them, along with articles and pamphlets describing domestic violence against men and the reasons behind it.

NCSC: Domestic Violence Resource Guide

www.ncsc.org/information-and-resources/browse-topics-a-z.aspx

This information is written for lawyers. Yet, this collection of annotated links from the National Center for State Courts offers useful information to anyone trying to resolve a domestic violence situation.

A Future for Marriage?

Since John Castellano's profession is helping people "uncouple," I asked him if his work has made him cynical about love.

"Not at all!" he said. He pointed out that he had recently married himself and had joyfully attended the wedding of his boss just prior to our interview. "In the end," he noted, "it just comes down to picking the right person."

This divorce lawyer was emphatic: "I still believe in marriage."

Part Two

Parenting

If all goes well with love, it may be time to add children into the mix. Unfortunately, as the saying goes, they do not come with operating instructions. That doesn't mean that you can't download the missing manual from the internet. Here are some resources to help you guide young people into adulthood.

5

In Development:
Pregnancy and Parenting on the Web

The unflattering name for those huge purses currently in fashion is "diaper bags." I remember the day when my son finally used his last pull-up diaper. I swore that I would never ever again haul around a diaper bag. And that is why even today, my hobo bag is a shrunken version of what is fashionable.

General Pregnancy and Parenting Sites

I gave up the business of making new people after my first came out so well. My boy was born in 1995, which was unfortunately before the web became the fountain of pregnancy and child rearing resources it is today. My husband and I floundered about, often unsure about the best way to rear our infant son. Today's new moms can find answers quickly using these sites.

iVillage: Parenting and Pregnancy
parenting.ivillage.com

The iVillage Parenting and Pregnancy site does everything for the expectant mom short of feeling the birth pangs. Whether you are trying to conceive, are pregnant, or have given birth (even 15 years ago—they have a teen parenting section), register for free to "personalize" your iVillage experience. Get customized baby calendars, weekly newsletters, a place to show your photos online, and advice from other moms. The comprehensiveness of this portal makes it a great place to start.

Pregnancy.org
www.pregnancy.org

Pregnancy.org is a general information site built "by parents for parents." Browse articles by volunteer experts about pregnancy and getting pregnant, infant care, and breastfeeding. Join for free to calculate your due date or to choose a baby name. Get advice from child psychologist Dr. Laura Markham. There are midwives and lactation consultants here, too.

BabyCenter
www.babycenter.com

This international site features articles written by experts about all stages of childrearing, even adoption advice. Visit the Pregnancy and Parenting Tool Directory to find helpful programs like the Ovulation Calculator, the Baby Name Explorer, and even a Potty Training Readiness Checklist. Register to track your pregnancy week by week. Also, get freebies and coupons for baby goods! Follow BabyCenter on Twitter and Facebook.

What to Expect When You're Expecting
www.whattoexpect.com

The print version of *What to Expect When You're Expecting*, by Heidi Eisenberg Murkoff, her mom Arlene Eisenberg, and sister, nurse Sandee Hathaway, has been the bible for pregnant moms since it was first published in 1984. It spawned a whole "expectant" franchise: *What to Expect: The First Year*, *The Toddler Years*, etc. (I'm waiting for a new title from the brand: *What to Expect: The Middle Ages*.) Read their "New Baby Basics" to find the same essential information for first time parents: instructions for the most essential tasks, like how to give the baby a bath. The books and the website are the missing manual for new people!

Pregnancy and Infant Health

Having a baby is not a disease, but it may count as a "condition," albeit a temporary one, requiring medical attention. Also, babies are bound to get sick as their new little immune systems encounter the germs of this world for the first time. Find reliable medical information to take with you to the doctor on these sites.

Mayo Clinic: Healthy Lifestyle

www.mayoclinic.com/health/HealthyLivingIndex/Healthy LivingIndex

Find current, authoritative answers to all pregnancy health questions from preconception to labor and delivery under the "Pregnancy" section. Check up on the kids in the Infants, Children, and Teen health areas.

March of Dimes: Pregnancy

www.marchofdimes.com/Pregnancy/pregnancy.html

The March of Dimes presents trustworthy articles not only on how to have a healthy pregnancy, but what to do if complications occur. There are tips about what to consume during pregnancy (folic acid, calcium) and what to avoid (alcohol, mercury, rodents).

CDC: Having a Healthy Pregnancy

www.cdc.gov/ncbddd/bd/abc.htm

The Centers for Disease Control and Prevention (CDC) offers 26 quick tips for a healthy pregnancy. Examples include advice to take folic acid and to get plenty of Zzzzs.

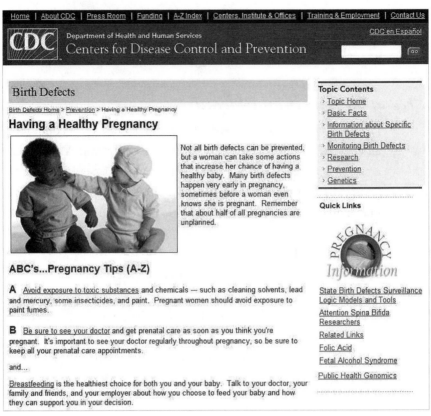

CDC: Having a Healthy Pregnancy

WomensHealth.gov: Healthy Pregnancy

www.womenshealth.gov/pregnancy

The National Women's Health Information Center offers reliable health information for pre-pregnancy, pregnancy, and tips for breastfeeding and finding child care.

American Association of Birth Centers

www.birthcenters.org

Don't want to give birth in a hospital? Visit this site to find a birth center near you. The American Association of Birth Centers also covers such issues as whether birth center expenses are covered by health insurance.

Healthy Children

www.healthychildren.org

Pediatricians from the American Academy of Pediatrics offer parents timely, reliable health information for every stage of their child's life completely free of commercial consideration. Register to automatically see the most relevant information for your child's age. Browse pediatricians' answers to questions sent in by users. Or, ask your own! Use this site to find a pediatrician in Canada or the U.S.

General Advice for New Parents

It's all coming back to me now. My son had wicked colic from his second week through his twelfth. Let's just say we watched a lot of foreign films during that time—because we could read the dialogue during the wailing. Here's a grab bag of advice sites to help new parents get through that first difficult year.

AskDrSears.com

askdrsears.com

Martha and William Sears, along with their sons Bob and Jim, are all experienced pediatricians and parents themselves. They offer professional advice on how to solve common baby problems, from breast feeding to sleep issues. Sign up for an email newsletter from the doctors Sears.

Colicky Baby? Read This Before Calling an Exorcist

sandrablakeslee.com/articles/colic_mar05.php

Did I say I wanted a child? When my high-strung infant screamed his lungs out for hours at a time, I sincerely doubted my decision. I wish that I could have read science writer Sandra Blakeslee's article outlining pediatrician Harvey Karp's five-step method for calming that psychosis-inducing bundle of joy. Karp's book, *The Happiest Baby on the Block* (Bantam, 2005), and accompanying DVD have, understandably, sold millions. Karp's website is www.happiestbaby.com.

BabyCenter: The Ferber Method Demystified

www.babycenter.com/0_the-ferber-method-demystified_7755.bc

Dr. Richard Ferber popularized the "crying it out a little at a time" method for teaching 4-to-6-month olds to soothe themselves to sleep in his book *Solve Your Child's Sleep Problems* (Fireside, 1986). I tell you frankly, when my son was an infant, "Ferberizing" saved our sanity. This approach to behavior change

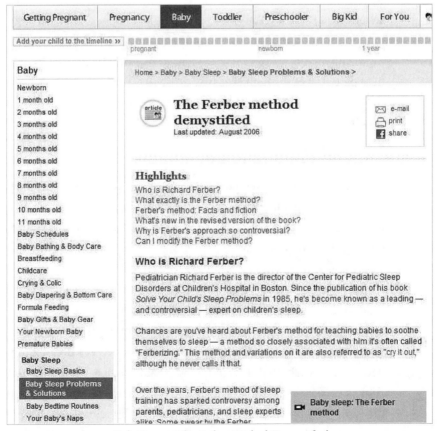

BabyCenter: The Ferber Method Demystified

is called "graduated extinction." It worked for our boy: He graduated into sleep, and we didn't go extinct. Read about it here.

Baby Name Wizard
www.babynamewizard.com

What's in a name? Find out at this jolly interactive site. The "Name Voyager" graphically shows the popularity of names over the decades, stacked in alphabetical order. Type in a name to track its history. Or, search for names by sound, syllable, and style (traditional, contemporary, and even non-standard spelling).

Social Security Administration: Popular Baby Names
www.ssa.gov/OACT/babynames

The Social Security Administration lists the most popular names in the U.S. all the way back to 1880. It also offers links to other useful government sites for children, such as tips for child-proofing a home, infant/child product recalls, and links to the WIC program from the U.S. Department of Agriculture.

FitPregnancy.com
www.fitpregnancy.com

Browse the articles in this online version of the magazine for tips on how to regain that pre-pregnancy fit physique, the one that was so attractive that it got you into this trouble in the first place!

Mothering Magazine
www.mothering.com

Mothering is the publication (print and online) for parents who want to live in a "natural" healthy way (i.e., it advocates breast-feeding, midwifery, and homeopathy). Visit the site to read free content about "health, personal, environmental, medical, and lifestyle issues." For fun, try the online Chinese Gender Prediction Calendar (www.mothering.com/interactive/chinesecalendar/gender predictor.html).

Breastfeeding

Not everyone has an easy time with breastfeeding. But I tell ya, I was a moo-cow momma for a couple of years! Here are some tips on how to do it, if you can and choose to.

La Leche League International

www.llli.org

The La Leche League is an international organization of mothers who have breastfed their babies and, in turn, try to help other mothers get the information and support they need to succeed in their own breastfeeding. Get help with breastfeeding questions, read about breastfeeding laws in your area, and listen to podcasts discussing various aspects of breastfeeding and mothering.

Medela Breastfeeding U.S.

www.medelabreastfeedingus.com

Medela, the Swiss breast pump company, offers breastfeeding and other tips for infant care. Medela even offers ways that can help an adoptive mother to breastfeed. Follow their advice and interact with other moms on Medela's Facebook page or Twitter feed.

Baby as Shopping Experience

Babies do need a lot of stuff: car seats, bassinets and cribs, changing tables, strollers, high chairs, not to mention diapers, formula, bottles, and clothes! Of course, you can borrow some things from your family and friends or buy them secondhand on eBay, on craigslist, or at yard sales. Still, there will be plenty of new things to buy ... on the web!

Diapers.com

www.diapers.com

Parents spend an average of $1,500 annually per child paying for disposable diapers. Buy diapers online from this site to have them delivered to your home. Set up an account to have diapers delivered automatically, free of shipping charges and taxes. The site estimates the annual cost of monthly diaper delivery to be just $500 per year, a 66 percent savings over retail. Find baby formula here too, along with baby gear of all kinds.

Babies "R" Us

www.babiesrus.com

This specialized division of Toys "R" Us offers all the things that babies need: gear, bathing and feeding supplies, safety products, toys, and clothing.

BreastPumps4Less

www.breastpumps4less.com

Buy breast pumps and accessories for the lowest prices on the web.

Pampers.com

www.pampers.com

Get free advice from the Pampers Parenting Institute. Join Pampers.com to get a chance to win a year's supply of diapers and training pants as well as free samples and a way to earn points toward children's merchandise in its Gifts to Grow rewards program.

Parenting Blogs

Why not get tips from savvy parents who are going through the same things as you? Follow these parenting blogs.

Parent Hacks

www.parenthacks.com

Computer writer Asha Dornfest compiles this blog, which overflows with clever ideas for managing very young people. Learn how life experiences such as getting a pet can teach social skills.

Get a deal on a car seat. Use search engines to teach spelling. The tips just keep on coming!

MommaSaid.net
www.mommasaid.net

Jen Singer, writer and mother of two boys, finds the funny in the funhouse of parenthood. For example, Singer is the force behind "*Please* Take My Children to Work Day" for stay-at-home moms.

Parenting Science
www.parentingscience.com

Do you need to switch breasts during feeding? How can you get children to eat new foods? What are proven methods for sleep training? The science-minded parent can turn to this blog written by biological anthropologist Gwen Dewar for answers.

DadLabs
www.dadlabs.com

Austin's Tony Lanier, Clay Nichols, and Brad Powell are "taking back paternity" with a blog and video site for new "super dads." DadLabs offers "humorous tips and advice from dads on parenting, fatherhood, children, and coping with wives and mothers." I particularly enjoyed Lanier's thorough review of front-loading washing machines. Subscribe to DadLabs podcasts on iTunes or have programs delivered to your RSS reader. Join the site to join in on the fathering forums.

Baby Apps

Apps are finding a place in the new parent toolbox. There are ovulation calculators, due date monitors, contraction timers, nursing trackers, and even games to occupy toddlers. Of course, one mom remarked that her favorite app was Solitaire, because she played it to amuse herself while nursing her infant! Here is a tiny sample from the exploding universe of baby apps.

BabyBump App

alt12.com/products

For about three dollars, download this complete pregnancy monitor. Get weekly updates on embryo development. Graph the size of your growing belly. Keep a journal. Finally, use the handy contraction tracker to know when to leave for the hospital. Also available for Android and Palm Pre.

iTunes: Nursing Master

itunes.apple.com/us/app/nursing-master/id356687268?mt=8

For $2, iPhone mamas and papas can track nursing time for baby (or babies!) with this app.

iTunes: Preschool Adventure

itunes.apple.com/app/preschool-adventure/id286526367?mt=8

Ninety-nine cents gets you six games that teach toddlers shapes, colors, and words. This is just one of an exploding universe of baby game apps that essentially turn the mobile into a handheld game console. Parents find these to be a great help to distract children while waiting in a restaurant, for example.

iTunes: Kideos

itunes.apple.com/app/kideos/id348733245?mt=8

This free iTunes app finds videos appropriate for specific age groups—down to age 0—to play on your iPhone or iPad. Play them on your big computer, too, on the regular website (www.kideos.com). Complete the free registration to block the ability to link through to inappropriate videos on YouTube.

Adoption

Not all families occur by chance. Some children are chosen specifically by adoptive parents well after they are born. The web offers help for these families that are built quite deliberately with love.

Adoption.com

Adoption.com

www.adoption.com

Visit this site to research all aspects of adoption, from how to adopt to advice for birth parents and those searching for them to plain general parenting advice. The Arizona-based site is "committed to helping as many children as possible find loving, permanent homes," particularly those special needs children who otherwise wouldn't be able to find families.

AdoptUsKids

www.adoptuskids.org

The Children's Bureau of the Administration for Children and Families (www.acf.hhs.gov/programs/cb) and the Department of Health and Human Services support this site, which seeks to place foster children in permanent homes. Use this site to learn how to become a foster parent or to adopt an older child, often one with special needs.

Hush, Little Baby

A library schoolmate, John Dobbins, now electronic resources librarian at Occidental College, and his wife, the Reverend Anne Cohen, fulfilled their dream of having a family by adopting a son.

When I asked Dobbins about web resources that he used for the baby, a few days passed before I received his reply. He apologized, explaining that his new son had "gone from waking us every 2 hours to every 3 hours or more, so that's progress."

Perhaps he was singing the boy to sleep. He wrote, "This morning I found some lullaby lyrics on Adoption.com (lullabies.adoption.com)."

Go to sleep my darling, close your little eyes.
Angels are above us, peeping through the skies.
God is in his heaven, and he watch doth keep.
Time for little children to go to sleep.

With the web and mobile apps helping all new moms and dads, we can all sleep like a baby.

6

Data Download:
Kids and Homework

Where I work, in the affluent community of San Marino, California, homework isn't so much a learning tool for students as it is a competitive sport for their parents.

When the library doors open at 10 AM, I am often confronted by svelte stay-at-home moms with master's degrees who have just received text messages from their little ones. "My son has to do a report on Mission San Luis Obispo," or "What do you have on the red-tailed fox?" or "I need exactly 200 pages on Cabeza de Vaca."

What do these parents—or, even better, their kids—do about homework when the library is closed? Turn on the computer, of course, and jump onto the internet. Fortunately, there is quite a bit of helpful, authoritative homework help out there on the open web, if you know where to look.

Educational Search Engines for Kids

We have heard that the web is a great place for kids to learn. But where to start? Search for answers using these directories of educational sites.

ipl2 for Kids

www.ipl.org/div/kidspace

You've got homework? Whether you are studying history, art, math, science, or sports, the librarians at ipl2 link to quality websites that have your answers. You can even ask a librarian a question online! This site is hosted by Drexel University.

KidsClick!

www.kidsclick.org

If knowledge is power, then this site is rocket fuel. KidsClick! is owned and run by the School of Library and Information Science at Kent State University, where they choose only the safest and most useful homework-helping sites for students from kindergarten through the seventh grade.

Yahoo! Kids

kids.yahoo.com

This commercial search starting point features movie trailers and games suitable for younger elementary school kids. Click on over to the "Study Zone" (kids.yahoo.com/learn) to find educational content. Yahoo! Kids used to be called Yahooligans!

General Homework Help

Need answers? Keep these homework sites handy to help out.

Discovery Education: Homework Help

school.discoveryeducation.com/homeworkhelp/homework_help_home.html

Children (and adults!) can watch short videos that explain the basics of math, writing, science, and social studies. Check the "Other" section for links to world language tutorials, computer training, and even music theory lessons.

Infoplease Almanac

www.infoplease.com

You can answer so many homework questions with this almanac/dictionary/atlas/encyclopedia bookmarked on your browser. Use the Infoplease tools: calculator, periodic table, place finder, and spell checker.

Fact Monster

www.factmonster.com

Here is the cartoony, "kid friendly" cousin to Infoplease Almanac. Use the dictionary or the encyclopedia. Browse topics such as Math and Money, Word Wise, or Homework Center. You can also search the site by keyword.

Library of Congress: For Kids and Families

www.loc.gov/families

Ask a simple question: "What is the strongest muscle in the body?" Get a page full of answers in return ("It depends on how you measure strength.") along with links to authoritative resources about human musculature. And that's just in the "Everyday Mysteries," aka science section. Learn about history, geography, and music and dance from this page. There's bound to be something here to help finish that school assignment.

Wikipedia

en.wikipedia.org

You heard me: Wikipedia. Yes, it is written and edited by users who may lack authority or want to sell their point of view. Still, it can be a useful homework jumping-off place, as long as everyone keeps a few critical thinking guidelines in mind. First, Wikipedia is best for non-controversial topics. Stay away from abortion on Wikipedia (that's all I'm sayin'). Second, it is great for very new subjects that haven't yet shown up in encyclopedias. When my husband was sick, I used it to research drugs for his cancer that

Library of Congress: For Kids and Families

were so new, they only had letters and numbers for names. Third, check out the bibliographies at the end of the articles. These lists often contain authoritative resources. Remember, no matter what source you use for your homework, double check to make sure that another one backs it up.

Reading and Writing

The web touts its images and video. Ironically though, much of it is still text-based. Think Twitter! Kids need to learn to read and write now more than ever. These sites may help.

Kidsreads.com

www.kidsreads.com

The K–6 crowd can visit this page to find out about favorite authors and book series. Read reviews of new books, or join a book club. There are book club guides for children's books with questions for discussion, just like Mommy's book group has.

AR BookFinder

www.arbookfind.com

Many schools use the Accelerated Reader (AR) program to judge the reading level of children's books and to test students on what they have read. Find the "AR points" of most children's books here.

ipl2 for Teens: A+ Research and Writing for High School and College Students

www.ipl.org/div/aplus

Kathryn L. Schwartz wrote this guide while a student of the Information and Library Studies program at the University of Michigan. It not only teaches writing skills but also how to research a paper using both print and online sources.

ipl2 Special Collections

www.ipl.org/div/litcrit

Having trouble figuring out the themes in that Steinbeck book? Look here to find analyses of writers and their works. If literary criticism is free anywhere on the web, the ipl2 has found it and categorized it by date, by genre, or alphabetically by author name.

CliffsNotes

www.cliffsnotes.com

The name may be synonymous with a big cheat, but really, the synopses offered by CliffsNotes can help students understand and remember what they have read. This "free" site is packed with ads,

CliffsNotes

but the complete content is here. Download analyses of individual titles to your iPhone for 99 cents, or listen to the free "Cram Casts" on the site or on iTunes. CliffsNotes also offers online study guides for science, math, and foreign languages.

Online Books Page

onlinebooks.library.upenn.edu

John Mark Ockerbloom, a digital library planner and researcher at the University of Pennsylvania, created and maintains this definitive, searchable directory to books freely readable over the web. Nothing new here, because he only links to full text in the public domain, that is, books published before 1923. On the other hand, you can pull up a copy of any classic you might need. Search by author, title, or Library of Congress subject heading. Find your Chekhov, Mark Twain, and Edith Wharton here!

Google Books

books.google.com

My son had to do a report on the 19th-century Scottish chemist Thomas Graham. Graham was a "zesty" worker, according to his peers, and he practically invented modern chemistry. Still, his personal life was little noted. Certainly, there are no contemporary full-length biographies of the man. What could my boy use as a resource besides the sketchy and short entry in Wikipedia? Google Books! On this site, we found a complete scan of a contemporary memorial to Graham, the print version of which is housed in a library at Harvard! Copyright restrictions keep post-1923 texts out of this database, but there is no better place to peruse earlier works.

Son of Citation Machine

citationmachine.net

Your paper is due, but you can't remember how to format web article entries in your bibliography. What do you do? Turn to the online application Son of Citation Machine. Simply enter the author, title, publication date, and other relevant information for web or print sources, and the site generates a perfectly formatted bibliographic entry. Or, if your source is a book, just enter its ISBN. You can then copy and paste the results into your end notes. Other online citation generators include EasyBib (www.easybib.com) and KnightCite (www.calvin.edu/library/knightcite).

Science

I remember my one and only science fair project. I glued a plastic drinking straw onto the skin of a balloon stretched across the mouth of an empty jelly jar. This was supposed to be a barometer. I don't recall that it worked at all, and needless to say, I didn't win

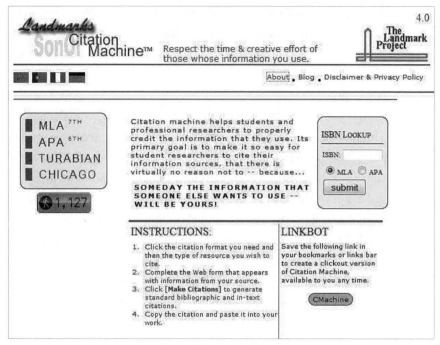

Son of Citation Machine

the science fair. But I kept that "barometer" in my room until its latex membrane crumbled.

Today, I would likely have a much more successful experience thanks to resources available on the web. Most students these days have to prepare projects for an annual school science fair. These lucky kids can access a wide variety of ideas, guidance, and up-to-date data on the internet. Here are some sites to help with experiments and other science-related reports.

Discovery Education: Science Fair Central

school.discoveryeducation.com/sciencefaircentral

Visit Discovery Education's guide to science fair projects. Receive guidance to the steps required in an experiment, get new ideas, and search their links and bibliographies for data.

ipl2 for Kids: Science Fair Project Resource Guide

www.ipl.org/div/projectguide

The librarians at ipl2 urge students not to panic about their science fair projects; just breathe and follow the step-by-step directions. The "Tools and Research" section links to quality science information appropriate for kids. Search ipl2 Kids for *science projects* to find links to other sites that offer guidance for science fair competitions.

Frank Potter's Science Gems

www.sciencegems.com

Physicist Frank Potter has maintained this unmatched collection of science sites for students since 1994. He has amassed more than 14,000 science resources and sorted them by category, subcategory, and grade level. He has three separate collections of physical science sites, two earth science subcategories, two on life science, and one each on mathematics and engineering. Search the lot of them by keyword, too.

How Everything Works

www.howeverythingworks.org

Louis A. Bloomfield, professor of physics at the University of Virginia, has been answering readers' questions regarding the physics of everyday things since 1997. Users can search Bloomfield's archive of revealed wisdom by keyword or topic. Find out why coffee seems warmer after you stir in cream, even though the cream is cold (transfer of energy). Discover the reason that paper towels absorb water (cellulose binds to water easily). And finally, uncover ways to make your cocoa so hot in the microwave that the cup explodes. Science is fun!

National Geographic Kids

kids.nationalgeographic.com

Younger elementary school children can learn about animals (for their animal report ... parents know the one I mean), countries, and the environment from this attractive site. Play educational games here, too!

NASA: For Students

www.nasa.gov/audience/forstudents

The Education Division of the National Aeronautics and Space Administration offers these pages designed to teach kids about space. Browse presentations and games by grade level, or use the search box to find specific information.

Neuroscience for Kids

faculty.washington.edu/chudler/neurok.html

Learn about nerves and the brain from Dr. Eric H. Chudler, neuroscientist at the University of Washington Engineered Biomaterials in Seattle. Search the site for answers, or browse topics, games, and quizzes.

MedlinePlus

www.nlm.nih.gov/medlineplus

Do you have to write a report on a rare disease? The National Library of Medicine has assembled an array of its resources onto one attractive portal, MedlinePlus, designed for general health consumers. Students can visit this site to find information on conditions, diseases, drugs, and wellness. Also, they can use the handy medical dictionaries here to translate difficult medical terms.

Social Studies and History

Sociology is the study of how people behave (and have historically behaved) in groups. Use these sites to learn about people and history.

History.com: History by Topic

www.history.com/topics

Search this A&E Television website to find concise synopses of (mostly) American historical events like World War II, the Abolitionist Movement, or the Boston Tea Party.

ClassBrain: State Reports

www.classbrain.com/artstate/publish

If you have a state report due, visit here first. ClassBrain provides maps, links to state sites, and interesting local lore from each congressional district. Print up the handsome templates to give a polished look to your report.

Houghton Mifflin Harcourt Education Place: Outline Maps

www.eduplace.com/ss/maps/world.html

The Houghton Mifflin Harcourt Education Place offers quality outline maps of the U.S., Europe, and the rest of the world free for homework use.

World History: HyperHistory Online

www.hyperhistory.com/online_n2/History_n2/a.html

HyperHistory covers 3,000 years of world history with an interactive combination of timelines, lifelines, and maps. Print copies of the timeline can be purchased through the site, or you can press *Shift/Print Screen* to copy and then paste the image into a document.

Biography.com

www.biography.com

Looking for people in history? Use this site to "search over 25,000 of the greatest lives, past and present." The site does not give in-depth information, but at least it will give you a handle on the subject of your biographical report and provide inspiration for further searches.

Math

Yes, I was the only drama major in the pre-med calculus class in college. But that was long ago. I must confess, in the decades since, I have never once had the opportunity to calculate the rate of change of the rate of change. So, when a student (or my son) asks for help with his or her math homework, I am often stumped. I turn to these sites for help.

Wolfram Alpha

www.wolframalpha.com

Here is an extraordinary new online factual computation engine. Enter any equation and get an answer at once, plotted on a graph, if necessary. But math is just the beginning with Wolfram Alpha. Enter your birth date to see what happened on that day. Enter your first name to gauge its popularity over time. Type in a place name to see its statistics. Download the free app to your iPhone or iPad.

Khan Academy

www.khanacademy.org

If you really cannot understand algebra, do yourself a favor and tune in to these lectures by MIT and Harvard graduate Salman Khan. In 15-minute segments, Khan walks you through the basics of arithmetic on up through calculus. His calm, clear explanations may save your grade. Check out his lectures on chemistry, biology, and even some history. Khan is a terrific teacher!

Protecting Kids Online

So much of the internet is unmitigated good. The free access to information on the web means that we and our children have the opportunity to learn more than anyone has ever known before. Still, the internet is not governed; like Nature herself, it is often beautiful and healing, yet wild with the potential to harm.

We can teach our children to connect safely by giving them some guidelines and helping them to think critically. Wise rules of thumb will help our kids to be not only knowledgeable but "knowledge-able," as Michael Wesch, professor of cultural anthropology at Kansas State University, calls it.

It's hard to know how to do that when our kids know more about the technology than we do. Here are ways to catch up and cope.

ConnectSafely

www.connectsafely.org

Larry Magid of SafeKids.com and Anne Collier of NetFamilyNews.org co-direct this organization, which offers up-to-date, easy-to-follow, sensible advice about establishing a family tech policy, for instance. This is a terrific place to keep up to speed with technologies as they emerge and perhaps pose new threats to the family.

Yahoo! Safely

safely.yahoo.com

Yahoo! teaches kids, teens, and parents techniques for staying away from predators and protecting privacy in the world of social networking.

BrainPOP Jr.: Internet Safety

www.brainpopjr.com/health/besafe/internetsafety

BrainPOP Jr. offers this free video that gives advice to children about what to do if they receive a message from someone they don't know. It also advises kids how to choose strong passwords and to avoid downloading programs without permission.

SafeKids.com

www.safekids.com

Syndicated columnist Larry Magid offers tips for kids and parents to help them avoid harm while using the web. He writes, "In this Web 2.0 world, kids aren't just consuming media, they're creating it and they have collectively embraced social media as a part of their lives. They don't go online; they are online—whether on a PC, a mobile device, a gaming console, or whatever comes next." Magid points out that the biggest online threats to kids come from themselves, when they disclose too much information, and from their peers, who may bully them.

Technology Is a Mirror

"The thing about this digital age is that it's holding up a very big, society-wide mirror to our faces nearly 24/7," writes Anne Collier on her NetFamilyNews blog (www.netfamilynews.org/2010/04/citizenship-social-web-mirror-in-our.html). In other words, technology is not really the problem. It simply shows us our problems, which are really behavioral and interpersonal.

"The central task of citizenship is learning how to be good to one another," writes Collier. "Let's do ourselves and our children a favor and not make it one bit more complicated than that."

Kindness online and plenty of learning: Sounds like a great way to grow up!

7

Higher E-ducation:
Websites for Teens and College

Ah, the transition from childhood to adulthood. This is a time fraught with opportunity as well as peril. My son, now in his mid-teens, is a crackerjack kid working toward a bright future. Still, there are times when I worry. We know that the prefrontal cortex of the brain, its decision-making center, doesn't fully develop until about age 25. My job: to keep my boy alive and flourishing until then.

A Parent's Guide to the Teen Brain
www.drugfree.org/teenbrain

The Partnership for a Drug-Free America answers the question, "Why does your teen do that?" Turns out, from age 13 to 25, the brain matures from the back to the front, strengthening some connections and permanently pruning those it doesn't use. For a few years, the amygdala reigns, raging with all its impulse and emotion. Finally, the judgment center behind the forehead comes into its own, but not until your kid is way out of college.

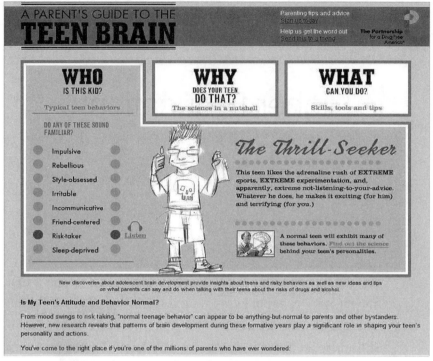

A Parent's Guide to the Teen Brain

Yikes! No wonder we hit the occasional rocky patch. Fortunately, there are resources on the web to ease the way as he transitions from high school to college and beyond.

Test Preparation

It seems that being a teen is all about testing. In addition to testing the limits of parents, teens must take tests to drive, to get out of high school, and to get into college. Here is some test prep help.

ipl2 for Teens

www.ipl.org/div/teen

Whether you need help with homework, college applications, or answers to embarrassing questions, the librarians at ipl2 have gathered high quality websites to get you the answers.

HippoCampus

www.hippocampus.org

Study for AP and other college entrance tests by clicking through the free multimedia lessons offered here. Subjects include algebra, calculus, American government, statistics, and psychology. Some tutorials are also offered in Spanish. The Monterey Institute for Technology and Education created this amazing resource.

DriversEd.com

driversed.com

Without question, one of the most important tests for any teen is the one that earns a driver's license. This attractive site offers lots of free state-specific traffic courses and interactive driving games. Taking official state tests through DriversEd.com (where available) costs about $100.

Educational Testing Service

www.ets.org

Although the College Board administers the SAT, the Educational Testing Service (ETS) actually writes it (along with the GRE, TOEFL, etc.). ETS also provides sample tests and ways to buy test prep materials. And, you can register for the SAT and the other tests via this site.

ACT Test Prep

www.actstudent.org/testprep

If you're taking the ACT, stop here to get tips for success. Go through the practice test questions all at once, or try the "ACT Question of the Day." Buy test prep materials here, too.

DriversEd.com

Planning for College

Every year high school seniors sweat out the wait for those fat letters of acceptance from the colleges of their choice. Congratulations to those who get them! How did they achieve their success? And how are they going to pay for their education? Planning ahead is the key. And the web has many sites that can help students and parents prepare for the day when the young ones leave the nest and fly to the halls of academe.

College Board

www.collegeboard.com

This comprehensive resource is the site for the College Board, which administers the all-important SAT test. You can register for the test here and put in lots of free practice, too. Do a school search to discover the entrance requirements of each college. Follow the timeline to know when you have to complete each piece of the puzzle that will get you into college. Use the scholarship search and financial aid planner to pay for it.

Peterson's

www.petersons.com

Peterson's, owned by private student loan company Nelnet, Inc., walks students and parents year by year through the college planning process, starting in the ninth grade. Users can search colleges and read about student aid and standardized tests. Subscribe to Peterson's emailed "Word of the Day" to build vocabulary for the SAT. Follow Peterson's on Facebook.

Adventures in Education

www.aie.org

Wow! The Texas Guaranteed Student Loan Corporation assembled this really useful site to help students decide on colleges, write effective applications, and figure out how to pay for their education. Search for scholarships and learn to properly fill out the dreaded FAFSA (Free Application for Federal Student Aid). There are also job hunting and money management tips.

XAP

www.xap.com

Sign up for a free account to access decision trees that help you pick a college and figure out how to pay for it. There is a financial aid "wizard," along with links for submitting college applications online. Also, you can set yourself on a satisfying career path with tests that assess your work values and interests.

Researching and Applying for College

We can find out so much about colleges by doing research online. And, once our kids pick their schools, they can apply over the web.

U.S. News & World Report: Education

www.usnews.com/sections/education

The Education section of the website of *U.S. News & World Report*, the (now monthly) news magazine, is a good place to start exploring college options. Browse its lists of "best" colleges for various courses of study. (Although its ranking methodology has been criticized, *U.S. News & World Report* does list the major players.) The site also offers articles about financing college, including a Financial Aid Letter Decoder to help you understand how your award stacks up. Another feature is the "Guide to Admissions" (www.usnews.com/education/best-colleges/features/guide-to-admissions), which addresses the tests, the admission essays, and the latest college admissions news.

University of Illinois at Urbana-Champaign:
College and University Rankings

www.library.illinois.edu/edx/rankings

The Education and Social Science Library at the University of Illinois at Urbana-Champaign assembled this directory of college-ranking services. It covers the main surveys (like the *U.S. News & World Report* rankings) as well as some more off-beat ones (for example, one ranking service that looks at colleges most friendly to those with disabilities).

College Prowler

collegeprowler.com

What is attending that particular school really like? Luke Skurman set up this site of college reviews for students by students. Register for free to see colleges ranked by "tons of different criteria" like athletics, campus dining, and the hotness of your fellow students.

Cappex

www.cappex.com

Cappex is kind of a dating service for college. You fill in your free profile. Colleges contact you if they are interested. After you enter your GPA and standardized test scores, use the "My Chances" calculator to see if it is worthwhile to apply at your favorite schools. See what scholarships or loans might best fit you based on your profile. Note: The loan section of the site is powered by a private student loan company.

The Common Application for Undergraduate Admission
www.commonapp.org

Nearly 400 public and private colleges across the U.S. accept the Common Application, which means that you only have to fill it out once. This app is for institutions that evaluate prospective students by "holistic" criteria, that is, they consider student essays, recommendations, and campus diversity in their selection processes along with test scores.

Applying for Financial Aid

With college costs so high, applying for financial aid may be a student's most important step.

FAFSA on the Web
www.fafsa.ed.gov

Filing a FAFSA is the first step for a family applying for financial aid. Get out your tax returns and bank statements: This is going to be an uncomfortably thorough financial examination. Still, the FAFSA can be the key to thousands of dollars in scholarships. After the FAFSA is processed, students receive their "Student Aid Report," or SAR, which summarizes the FAFSA. The SAR is sent to the colleges of their choice. The schools award aid by comparing their COA (cost of attendance) to the family's EFC (expected family contribution). LOL, this is alphabet soup!

FinAid! The Smart Student Guide to Financial Aid

www.finaid.org

Mark Kantrowitz created this most comprehensive page of student financial aid articles and links. Visit this site to learn all there is to know about scholarships and other financial aid.

Fastweb

www.fastweb.com

This excellent free service asks applicants to fill out an extensive online questionnaire about their interests and experiences, as well as those of their parents. Then, it matches these characteristics to a huge database of scholarships. When new scholarships appear that fit a profile, Fastweb sends an email to notify students about it. It also can automatically print out a scholarship query letter. All a student has to do is sign it and pop it in the mail. Cool!

College Board Scholarship Search

apps.collegeboard.com/cbsearch_ss/welcome.jsp

Register with the College Board to search its database of more than 2,300 sources of college funding.

ManagingCollegeCost.com

managingcollegecost.com

Parents, in return for free registration, get guidance counselor Frank Palmasani's video seminars about how to pay for your children's college education. Keep up to date with the latest developments in financial aid with Palmasani's blog.

Career Planning?

We used to assume our working lives would be linear. We would decide what we want to be when we grow up, go to school to get the skills, and then begin our ascent in our chosen careers.

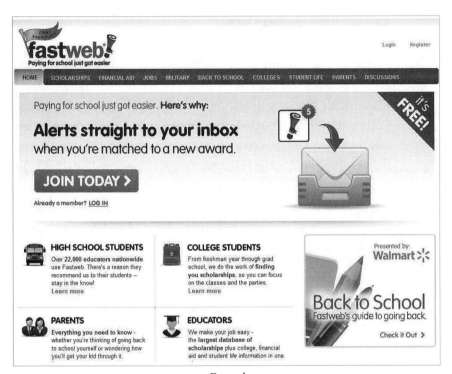

Fastweb

Recent studies show, however, that career paths are rarely straightforward. Parents, are you working at the job that you saw for yourself at age 18? Neither am I. (That's okay. I was wrong.)

This is the natural way of things. As Jim E. H. Bright and Robert G. L. Pryor put it, "It is increasingly accepted that career behavior is influenced by unplanned and chance events to a much more significant degree than has been typically acknowledged."[1]

In other words, we should take our best guess, move forward, and stay alert for unexpected opportunities.

Still, it's not a bad idea to have some clear idea of our strengths and tendencies to see where they might match up with majors and career paths. Here are some sites that may help.

Keirsey Temperament Sorter

keirsey.com

Are you a "champion?" or a "provider?" Dr. David Keirsey, author of *Please Understand Me: Character and Temperament Types* (with Marilyn Bates, 5th ed., Prometheus Nemesis Book Co., 1984), has mounted this online version of the Keirsey Temperament Sorter-II (KTS-II) test, related to the classic Myers-Briggs Type Indicator, which classifies personalities into 16 Jungian personality "types," or temperaments. In return for free registration, receive a short analysis. A full report runs from $5 to $20. The AdvisorTeam explains the four temperaments (www.advisorteam.org/the_four-temperaments).

Personality Pathways

www.personalitypathways.com/type_inventory.html

Here is a super-quick (and cheaper) version of the Myers-Briggs Type Indicator test.

Personal SWOT Analysis

www.mindtools.com/pages/article/newTMC_05_1.htm

What are your strengths? What do you need to work on to achieve your goals? What are the advantages and disadvantages of pursuing a major or a career? Sometimes, writing it out makes the situation clearer. Try the SWOT (Strengths, Weaknesses, Opportunities, and Threats) technique described here to help you decide what path to follow.

Bureau of Labor Statistics Occupational Handbook

www.bls.gov/oco

Now that you understand yourself a little better, the next question is: What jobs might suit your strengths? The U.S. Bureau of Labor Statistics provides this amazing resource that tells you all the jobs that exist, what training you need to do them, and trends and outlooks for these positions.

Apps for Teens

Kids know so much more about cell phone apps than we adults ever will. They already spend hours a day thumb-typing on Facebook and Twitter. Here are a handful of other apps that might be useful.

DriveSafe.ly
www.drivesafe.ly

It is so dangerous for teens to text while they drive. Still, many will do it anyway. Have yours download this free mobile app that will read cell phone messages aloud while they drive. The free version handles 25 words of a message; the paid version, at about $14 per year, allows up to 500 words per message and will speak in a male or female voice at variable speeds. Available for BlackBerry, Android, and, of course, iPhone.

iTunes: College Admissions Calculator
itunes.apple.com/us/app/college-admissions-calculator/id 337860002?mt=8

What are your chances of being accepted by the college of your choice? Find out with this $2 iPhone app. It is also available as an Android download for the same price.

iTunes: GrubHub Food Delivery
itunes.apple.com/app/grubhub-com/id302920553?mt=

Dining hall got you down? Visit GrubHub (www.grubhub.com) to see who delivers to the dorm or use this free iPhone app.

Once You're In

Once you've actually started your university career, the web becomes even more helpful. Here are several useful sites to get you started.

RateMyProfessors.com

ratemyprofessors.com

College students use the frank RateMyProfessors.com to help
them choose their classes. Leslie Fields, monitor at Crowell Public
Library, says, "This site was *so* helpful to me when I was in
school. It helped me to avoid bad teachers or to see if they taught
one class better than others." (Apparently, some professors are
more effective when instructing small upper-level seminars than
they at inspiring a large survey class.) "I used this all the time!" she
declares. These days, Fields could rate her instructors via cell
phone with the free iPhone app (itunes.apple.com/us/app/rate-my-
professors/id345381821).

Box.net

www.box.net

Forget the flash drive. Box.net gives you a free gigabyte of storage out in the "cloud." Upload your important files to Box.net.
Because they are on the web and not on your computer, you can
retrieve them wherever you happen to be working. You can also
share your files for easy collaboration on group projects. This site
is an essential tool for students.

Dropbox

www.dropbox.com

Even better than Box.net is Dropbox, a drop-dead essential for
all students and grownups who share files between computers.
This free program works on PCs, Macs, Linux, and smartphones
(Blackberry, iPhone, and Android). Simply install it on all your
devices and register with the site. Now you can drag a file that you
want to save from your desktop and into the Dropbox "cloud," that
is, their collection of big computers that are connected to the web.
There it sits until you log in again from any of your Dropbox-
enabled computers or phones. Users get 2 GB of storage for free;
50 or 100 GB can be had for $10 or $20 per month, respectively.

You can share files with other Dropbox users or invites others to join Dropbox if they're not users. Use Dropbox when you are on a private computer; Box.net, which works over the web, is better when you are using a public or shared computer.

Half.com
www.half.ebay.com

eBay established this site to help students buy and sell used books.

AddALL
www.addall.com

Singapore-based AddALL searches the entire web for the lowest online prices for new or used books.

Go Ask Alice!
www.goaskalice.columbia.edu

My teen may have questions about touchy topics like sex or alcohol that he doesn't want to ask me … or that I don't have answers for. I trust Go Ask Alice! from the Health Services department of Columbia University, to furnish him with unbiased, quality information about emotionally charged subjects.

How Did We Manage?

It's the funniest thing: My son seems to me so much smarter, wiser, and more sure of himself than I ever was at his age (or even *now*). He will achieve his goals early and spend a lot less time than I did thrashing around, wondering what he should do with his life.

I wonder if the information on the web helped him to become the smarty-pants that he is today. Would it have helped me to be surer of myself back then?

We'll never know. But I'm sure glad we have these tools now to help our kids succeed!

Endnote

1. Jim E. H. Bright and Robert G. L. Pryor, "The Chaos Theory of Careers: A User's Guide," *Career Development Quarterly* 53.4 (June 2005): 291.

Money and Home

Regardless of your relationship
status, as an adult, you need a
place to live and a way to
support yourself. Not easy in
these tough economic times!
Fortunately, the web offers tons
of advice for finding work,
saving money, and making sure
that your ride and your dwelling
remain in good repair.

8

E-Buy:
Shopping and Saving

Annual income twenty pounds, annual expenditure nineteen and six, result happiness. Annual income twenty pounds, annual expenditure twenty pounds ought and six, result misery.
—Charles Dickens, *David Copperfield*, 1849

Money makes the world go 'round, but recently the global economy has been juddering. Not enough liquidity! All of us have gotten at least a little dizzy from the effects. Many have lost jobs and homes. Even in the affluent city of San Marino, California, where I work, people have had to tighten their fiscal belts.

Yet, the web can help us stay resilient and cope when times are tough. How? By finding the lowest prices on things we need to buy and giving us free tools and advice for making the most of our money.

Shopping Search

You've heard the old joke, about how the shopping habits of modern women and men resemble those of our hunter-gatherer ancestors.

Men are (in general) the hunters: "Me want shirt. Get shirt. Go home." Whereas, we women tend to linger, gathering colorful objects and collecting them in our baskets.

The web enhances and intensifies our shopping proclivities. A man can search Amazon.com to find a book or a razor, click to buy, and it's on its way to his mailbox. A shopper gal like I am can invest hours to find the best deal on the most obscure item. Do you know how hard it is to find a solar-powered, radio-controlled watch designed for a woman?

Jeff Bezos started the web shopping revolution when he began selling books on Amazon in 1995. Now, his site is the go-to shopping spot for everything that can be shipped in a box. Google Products (www.google.com/products) is another great way to compare products and prices.

Coupons and Promotion Codes

In addition to basic product search engines, there are sites that search for coupons and promotional codes. One commentator gave this advice when checking out at an online store: "When I come across one of those 'promotion code' fields, I just Google the store and 'promotion code' or 'coupon.' Usually one of the first two or three links has a useful code."

RetailMeNot

www.retailmenot.com

This king of online coupon sites was founded by Australian web designer Guy King. Users submit the promotion codes that they find, often 200–300 per day. It's always a good idea to check RetailMeNot for discount codes before you make any online purchase. There are printable grocery coupons here, too.

Slickdeals.net

slickdeals.net

Sign up to find bargains and coupons on a variety of consumer electronics, home accessories, and computer games. Tera Forrest, master shopper and youth services librarian at Crowell Public Library in San Marino, California, uses Slickdeals.net to find discounts on Black Friday, the day after Thanksgiving that sets off the Christmas shopping season. Says Forrest, "It's like RetailMeNot on speed." Users register their opinions of deal values with thumbs up or down. Follow the site on your mobile browser (m.slickdeals.net).

BradsDeals
www.bradsdeals.com

Brad Wilson, a super searcher since his days back at the University of North Carolina, and his staff hand pick the best discounts off the web and deliver them to your inbox.

FatWallet
www.fatwallet.com

FatWallet helps us save money by offering coupons and rebates, handpicked deals from a variety of merchants, and forums where we can discuss our finds (after registering for free with the site, of course).

Gift Card Granny
www.giftcardgranny.com

Gift Card Granny collects deals on gift cards. That's right. It's like paying less money for money. "Granny" is in the same "Frugals" family as Coupon Sherpa (www.couponsherpa.com), Mrs. Sweepstakes (www.mrssweepstakes.com), and Mr. Free Stuff (www.mrfreestuff.com).

About.com: Coupons and Bargains
couponing.about.com

Journalist and retailer Donna Montaldo collects links to coupons and bargains from across the web.

Shopping Apps

The smart phone revolution is particularly useful for shopping: mobile internet plus a camera photo of a UPC code equals instant search for the best prices. Consequently, there are billions of shopping apps for the iPhone and others. Here's a sample.

SnapTell

www.snaptell.com

This free app for Android and iPhone lets users scan bar codes of books and DVDs with their camera phones. It then provides information about the scanned item as well as a price comparison search. SnapTell was purchased by Amazon, and so it's easy to make a purchase through Amazon with this app.

Coupon Sherpa: Mobile Coupons

www.couponsherpa.com/mobile-coupons

iPhone users, quit schlepping those heavy paper coupons. Download this free app to your phone. Find the coupon for your product or store, and the phone will display the coupon UPC code that the cashier can scan at checkout. Voila! Discount.

Google Goggles

www.google.com/mobile/goggles

Here is a multifunctional free app for Android phones. Its basic aim is to allow for an image-based web search via cell phone camera. Take a photo of the Statue of Liberty, and Google Goggles replies with information about it. Take a picture of a UPC code, and you find price comparison results from across the web.

Discount Stores and Services

These off-price stores pick up excess inventory and then pass the savings on to us.

Overstock.com

www.overstock.com

Utah-based Overstock.com sells excess quantities of everything from appliances to tiny beads for jewelry making. As they only charge $2.95 for shipping, I have found that best deals from Overstock are their area rugs: large, heavy area rugs of fairly high quality and a good price, delivered right to your door for three bucks. Overstock also specializes in luxury bedding for cheap. I bought a thick foam mattress-topper from them, too. The site also offers auctions on automobiles and items in bulk. Shop on the go by downloading the free Overstock app to your Android or iPhone (www.overstock.com/mobile) or punch in its regular web address on your mobile browser. The site comes to you automatically configured for the smart phone screen.

Woot!

woot.com

What fun is Woot! Founded by electronics wholesaler Matt Rutledge in 2004, the site usually offers one deal per day (usually a home electronic item) accompanied by snappy copy. Occasionally, there are "Woot! Off" days in which a series of items, often of high value, come up for sale. This site is great fun to visit, whether or not you are in the market for the item being offered. Shipping is always $5. Sister sites are Kids.Woot, Sellout.Woot, Wine.Woot, and Shirt.Woot. Sign up on-site to join the discussion as to whether the current Woot is a smart buy. Follow Deals.Woot (deals.woot.com) to see what web-wide deals other Woot! members have found and reported.

Sierra Trading Post

www.sierratradingpost.com

Anyone with an active lifestyle will appreciate the discounted brand-name merchandise offered by Wyoming's Sierra Trading Post. There are clothes and gear for fitness and outdoor adventures, such as cycling, camping, snow sports, and water sports, for men, women, and kids. Sign up to have deals delivered to your email.

Goldstar

www.goldstar.com

Before you buy tickets for live entertainment events in large U.S. cities, visit Goldstar. They sell heavily discounted excess seats for all the big shows in town: sporting events, theater, museums, and even the circus. Get a free membership and have upcoming event notifications sent to your inbox.

Groupon

www.groupon.com

Here is a curious exercise in group buying. Every day, Groupon presents one discount deal in the metropolitan area of your choice. These are discounts on shopping, services (like spas), events, or restaurants. Each deal requires a minimum number of buyers. If you choose to buy that day's deal, you enter credit card information. If enough people join you, your purchase goes through; if not, the deal is off. This sets up psychological incentive for you to get your friends to join the buying frenzy. Ingenious or nefarious? The service is free, so it costs nothing to find out!

The Dealmap

www.thedealmap.com

Search The Dealmap by location to see discounts offered by brick-and-mortar retailers and restaurants near you, displayed on a map. The Dealmap is a "mashup" of coupons that can simply be printed and deals offered through Goldstar and Groupon, which require a separate registration to use.

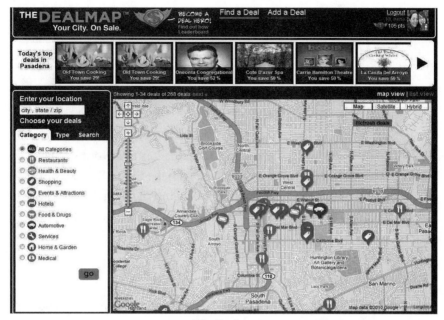

The Dealmap

GasBuddy.com

www.gasbuddy.com

Use this site to find the cheapest gas in your ZIP code, and see the prices displayed on a map. Find cheap gas on a cell phone browser with GasBuddy Mobile (gasbuddytogo.com) or via a text message (www.gasbuddy.com/gb_mobile_instructions.aspx). iPhone users can download the app for about three bucks (itunes.apple.com/app/gas-buddy-cheapest-gas-in/id299969005?mt=8).

Quality Check

Here are some tools for evaluating the quality of goods and retailers.

ConsumerSearch

www.consumersearch.com

You need a washing machine, a mattress, a laptop. How can you tell which are the best? ConsumerSearch reviews the reviews to point you in the right direction. For computers, it scans CNet.com; for appliances, it scans ConsumerReports.org. It picks the appropriate review resources for you and collates their findings. And it is completely free!

Better Business Bureau
www.bbb.org

How can you tell if an online merchant is trustworthy? One way is to see if the retailer is registered with the Better Business Bureau and if there are any complaints against it. Tera Forrest always checks the reputation of a seller at BBB. "If they're not on there, I won't buy from them," she asserts.

Budgeting and Saving Tools

Of course, we can't buy things unless we have money. The first step in managing our finances is to create a budget, so we can get a clear picture of our situation. Also, we should save a little bit out of every paycheck (if we're lucky enough to have one). Here are tools to help.

Mint.com
www.mint.com

Sign up to track your fiscal health on this free, web-based, personal finance manager. After users enter information about their credit card, investment, and banking accounts, Mint.com will analyze spending and offer savings ideas. The site is secure, as it is backed by VeriSign and the TRUSTe Privacy Seal Program. Get the free app for the iPhone (itunes.apple.com/app/mint-com-personal-finance/id300238550?mt=8) and Android phones, too.

The Beehive: Money
www.thebeehive.org/money

Let's face it: We're not born knowing how to handle money. The One Economy Corporation starts from the beginning, explaining

Mint.com

how to get a credit card, for example. The site's Budget Builder tool (www.thebeehive.org/money/spend-it/budget/budget-builder-tool) can help anyone to track their money. There are some tasty tax tips here, too.

BillShrink
www.billshrink.com

Visit BillShrink to get recommendations for the best credit cards, gas stations, savings banks, and cell phone plans for your lifestyle. When you sign up for a free account, BillShrink will email you when even better offers become available.

Bankrate.com: Find a Credit Card
www.bankrate.com/credit-cards.aspx

Bankrate.com offers terrific general advice for saving money. Use its credit card finder tool to discover one that will give you the best deal.

SmartyPig
www.smartypig.com

Saving toward a goal? Open an account with SmartyPig! Set it up to collect a certain amount from your checking account automatically each month. You won't even miss it! Meanwhile, your SmartyPig account grows and earns interest. Share your savings goals with others; they can even contribute. Then withdraw funds using a debit card. SmartyPig is powered by West Bancorporation (NASDAQ: WTBA).

AnnualCreditReport.com
www.annualcreditreport.com

Good credit is a basis for healthy personal finances. Monitor your vitals with AnnualCreditReport.com, the only site to offer free reports from the three major credit monitoring companies: Equifax, Experian, and TransUnion. Each compiles an individual's information and then issues a credit rating, called a FICO score (named after the company that initiated the scoring, Fair Isaac Company). The reports are free, but your actual FICO score will cost you.

Budgeting Blogs

Lots of folks are writing on the web about how to wrestle with personal finances. Turn to these blogs and newsletters for advice about how to invest, save money, and eliminate debt.

The Simple Dollar
www.thesimpledollar.com

Trent Hamm bounced back from a financial meltdown in his late 20s by examining all his expenses and reducing frivolous spending. Read his tips for spending less here, or have them sent to your email. "Trent's 14 Money Rules" include "Stop Wasting Time" and "Spend Less than You Earn." Thanks, Trent. Your lessons are timeless, but you sound like my dad!

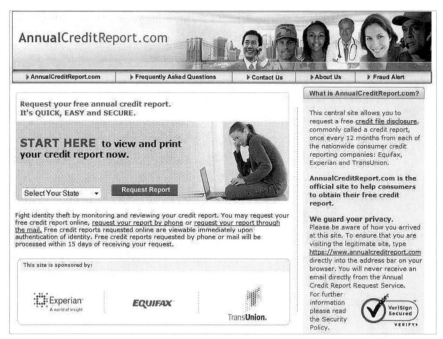

AnnualCreditReport.com

Get Rich Slowly

www.getrichslowly.org

In 2004, J. D. Roth of Portland, Oregon, had $35,000 of consumer debt. No longer! Follow Roth's blog for tips to do as he did: Eliminate debt and establish a positive cash flow.

Wise Bread

www.wisebread.com

The bloggers at Wise Bread are all about "living large on a small budget." Get tips on deals, living green, saving money, and earning more. Browse their library of personal finance and frugal living guides. Visit the site every day or follow them on Facebook or Twitter.

MoneySavingMom.com

moneysavingmom.com

Crystal Paine is a mother of three who revels in pinching pennies while raising her family. Paine's biggest help? Links to local grocery store weekly deals with coupons.

MashupMom.com

www.mashupmom.com

Hooray for Rachel Singer Gordon! She used to be a librarian, but now she devotes her finding skills to helping cash-strapped families. Through her blog, the author of *Point, Click, and Save: Mashup Mom's Guide to Saving and Making Money Online* (Information Today, Inc., 2010) links to print coupons, digital coupons (for downloading), and giveaways. Sign up to have her deal alerts delivered to your inbox or Twitter feed. Read her thoughts on how to make money by working from home. Gordon makes saving look fun!

Prosperity Place

www.sotkin.com/free_articles.php

Get personal finance advice with a New Mexico twist! Joan Slotkin mixes "Emotional Freedom Techniques" (www.sotkin.com/eft) with a dose of Hopi spiritualism to help readers of her newsletter reframe their thinking and improve their "relationship with money."

Can Money Make Us Happy?

Money can't buy happiness, or so the saying goes. But recent research shows that, contrary to the received wisdom, if you are poor, money will increase your happiness a lot, although the return on investment decreases as you get more comfortable (bpp.wharton. upenn.edu/betseys/papers/Happiness.pdf).

Where can you find more money saving and investment information? At your local library, of course, where all of that advice is absolutely free.

I hope that these money-saving tools help us all to increase our wealth and therefore, to a degree, our happiness!

9

Hardware:
D.I.Y. and Home Improvement on the Web

It's Sunday evening. Three loads of wash are finished and the dishwasher is running. My son is in the bathtub. Somebody flushes and … blub, blub. Smelly brown fluid burps backward up the drains.

Oh shoot. What am I supposed to do now?

Stuff Nobody Told You

Anyone who has ever owned a house (or been an adult responsible for any living space) has had to deal with home maintenance and repairs. I assume that men pass on knowledge of hammering and wiring to their sons. My father, a Fabulous Fifties kind of Pop, never breathed a word about dwelling repair to any of his five daughters. (What? The sinks of girls don't clog?) Because of my upbringing, the only thing I know about plumbing is what I learned from my mom: Pour a bottle of Liquid-Plumr (www.liquid-plumr.com) down the drain, wait an hour, douse with hot water, and hope for the best.

This lack of knowledge and experience is a big problem for my sisters and me. We are grown-ups now, and our children look to us for answers when things go wrong in the home. And heck, who wants to spend $200 for a professional to do a job that you could do yourself for $13.99?

The big problem comes when we have no idea how to make a repair or even what tools we might need to do the job properly. I'm not stupid; I can read directions as well as anyone. But many installation guides assume that we already know the tricks of the trade and so neglect to pass them on, just as fathers did to their daughters so many years ago.

An example: When he was about seven, my son, mistaking himself for a gymnast and the bathroom sink for a pommel horse, propelled his full weight into the air and down upon the edge of this delicate wall-mounted basin. We heard a crack. The drainpipe of the pedestal washstand snapped in two.

This should have been easy enough to fix. Yet, this Fix-It Chick decided that perhaps she should replace the entire faucet instead of just the pipe. "Can I install this myself?" I asked the plumbing supply salesman. "Sure," he assured me. "Just follow the directions."

The old faucet came out, and the new one went in just fine. Granted, it took me all day to do the job. Finally, in the evening, I slowly opened the water valves to test my handiwork. Liquid jets spurted from every joint! No one told me that I needed a special tool called a basin wrench to tighten the hard-to-reach connectors up under the sink.

Did I learn about the basin wrench from the plumber who charged $200 to tighten my screws the next day? No. I got that information after the fact off the web from sites designed to help us all repair and maintain our homes.

Home Improvement

Do-it-yourself home improvement and repair is big business. It appeals strongly to our American sense of self-reliance and the pioneering spirit. Warehouse home improvement stores have grown rich off this deeply rooted tendency and have a big stake in teaching their customers how to use the tools and supplies that they sell. Specialty magazines and television shows also have sites that support their message of construction and repair. Here is a hearty selection of the major ones.

Home Depot: How-To Center

ext.homedepot.com/how-to/how-to.html

Here you'll find instructions for installing, planting, painting, and repairing things around the home. If only I had watched the video about how to install a faucet before I began work on my bathroom sink, I could have finished the job with professional polish—and an intact bank account. Maybe.

Lowe's: How-To Projects

www.lowes.com/cd_How+To+Library_615580068_

Lowe's Home Improvement offers a library of instructions and videos for home repair and improvement. One particular project (www.lowes.com/cd_Replace+a+Faucet_515512929_) details the use of the mysterious basin wrench and assures us that the faucet swap should take no more than an hour. (I couldn't even get the water turned off in that amount of time.)

Ron Hazelton's House Calls: Home Improvement Online

www.ronhazelton.com

Ron Hazelton, host of his own home improvement television show, offers tips for facing common problems encountered by the inexperienced Fix-It Chick or Chap. For example, Hazelton reveals the mystical knowledge for extracting stripped screws: "The secret is a tool called a retractor. You use it with a handle, which you usually buy separately." Who knew?

Hometime.com: How-To Articles

www.hometime.com/Howto/projectlist.htm

Hometime has been running on PBS for decades. Click down through the subject list of "how-to" articles to find the information

Removing the Old Faucet

The most difficult part of replacing a faucet is removing the old one. Once the old stuff is out of the way, your nice new faucet should go in easily.

Step 1: Shut off the water. You can turn off the main water valve, or turn off the two valves immediately under the faucet you are replacing. Then, open the faucet and allow it to drain and release any pressure.

Step 2: Disconnect the water supply lines. If you choose not to replace the lines, disconnect them from the faucet only. If you choose to replace them, disconnect the lines from the shutoff valve. Actually, you might as well change them now since you are going to the trouble of replacing the faucet. It could save you an extra trip under the sink later.

Step 3: Remove the faucet from the sink. Basically, faucets are mounted in one of two ways–Bottom mount faucets are removed from above. For these, the handles and escutcheons must be removed to get to the nuts which secure the faucet in place. Top mount faucets are held in place by nuts located underneath the sink, and must be removed from below. The nuts may be loosened using waterpump pliers or a special basin wrench. The basin wrench is necessary when the area in which the nut is located is too tight to allow the use of pliers.

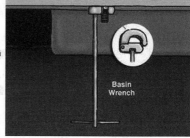

Basin Wrench

If it is an old sink and the nuts are rusted or corroded in place, apply penetrating oil and allow it to work into the threads before trying to remove the nuts.

Once the faucet has been removed, a buildup may be present on the sink in the area where the faucet plate or escutcheons were attached. Clean it off to make ready for the new faucet. A 50-50 solution of vinegar and water will help dissolve the buildup. Scrape it away with a razor blade and/or scouring pad.

Back to Top

Lowe's How-To Projects

that you need. There is an emphasis on new installation here, with overviews about the function of trap drains, for example.

Popular Mechanics: Home Improvement

www.popularmechanics.com/home/improvement

Popular Mechanics, a magazine famous for catering to the serious amateur, throws something to the less apt among us with its home improvement tips. Browse advice for interior and exterior enhancements, gardening, plumbing, energy efficiency, and home security.

Old House Web: How To Advice

www.oldhouseweb.com/how-to-advice

Painting, plumbing, wiring, even cleaning: The experts at Old House Web have something to say about all of it. Did you know that dust holds odor? A good reason to wipe it away every week.

There are forums on the site where you can post your own renovation questions.

Handy Guys Podcast

www.handyguyspodcast.com

Vrmm, vrrrm! Brian and Paul, the Handy Guys, offer advice for keeping the home in top shape. Learn about electrical issues, plumbing, and nailguns, among many other things, from their articles and podcasts. They even discuss their favorite DIY books. Ask your personal home maintenance question on their site. Brian and Paul may address your problem in their next podcast, which you can get via email, RSS feed, iTunes, or Twitter. They have helpful videos, too.

Handy Guys Podcast

BobVila.com: Home Improvement

www.bobvila.com/sections/home-improvement

Browse the Home Improvement section to find articles and videos on how to fix or install things around the home. The site offers quick tips for attractive yet inexpensive remodeling.

DIY: Do It Yourself Network

www.diynet.com

Find terrific articles and videos here about building new enhancements for the home as well as making home repairs. There is even a whole section about how to unclog the toilet (www.diynetwork.com/topics/toilets/index.html). DIY is a sister cable channel of the Food Network and HGTV (Home and Garden Television), all children of the Ohio-based Scripps Howard Broadcasting Company.

HGTV: Home Improvement

www.hgtv.com/home-improvement

Get advice from HGTV about painting, remodeling, and plumbing. HGTV also offers tips on crafts, organizing, and living "green."

Appliances, Tools, and Cleaning

On that unhappy Sunday evening when our drains backed up, I drove to the store and bought a couple of bottles of drain opener. Hours—and many bubbling tea kettles of water later—the bathtub slowly glurked empty. My family could finally use the bathroom—as long as we didn't run any other water at the same time.

The next day, the plumber informed us that our avocado tree had shoved its root through our 90-year-old cesspool line. (No wonder the fruit from that tree tasted so good the last couple of years!) It was clear that we would have to invest big bucks and get a professional to connect us to the city sewer.

A couple of evenings after our sewer line was redirected, I started the dishwasher and went to bed. A half an hour later, I heard my husband yell. The kitchen floor was flooded with hot water spewing from the base of the dishwasher!

We needed to clean up fast and get the dishwasher fixed. But first, we leapt onto the computer to check the web for help.

RepairClinic.com
www.repairclinic.com

Need to repair an appliance? Check here first! This site explains how the appliances in your house work and how to fix them. You can even order the parts you need here.

Toolcritic.com
www.toolcritic.com

We need to buy tools to fix our houses and appliances. How can we find the best? Visit Toolcritic.com to read reviews for saws, sanders, and drills, written by skilled enthusiasts. After you try a new tool, contribute your own review.

Housekeeping Channel
www.housekeepingchannel.com

The first step in home improvement may be a good wash up. This extremely well-organized site offers an abundance of advice and reviews about housekeeping and cleaning products written by celebrity names in home maintenance. Read tips on subjects ranging from doing laundry to finding time and motivation for cleaning. Have cleaning tips sent to your RSS newsreader daily.

Jeff Campbell's Clean Team: Speed Cleaning Rules and More
www.thecleanteam.com/rules.cfm

Jeff Campbell, one of America's leading home cleaning experts, and his "Clean Team" offer rules from their books about how to clean things quickly, guidelines for keeping a home clutter free,

Speed Cleaning Rules - From our book *Speed Cleaning*

Rule Number 1: Make every move count. That means work around the room once. Don't backtrack. It also means you must carry your equipment and supplies with you so you don't make dozens of aggravating trips back and forth across the room. Walk around the room once and you're done, except for the floor.

Rule Number 2: Use the right tools. Ah! Here's probably the major timesaver of the bunch. Give your specialized gadgets to your enemies. You need real tools that cut time to shreds. Most of all, you need a *cleaning apron* to hang tools on and store cleaning supplies in as you move around the room. The method depends on it, and soon you'll feel lost without yours.

Rule Number 3: Work from top to bottom. Dirt follows the laws of gravity just like anything else. When you start at the top and work to the bottom, you won't be constantly re-cleaning surfaces with dirt from above.

Jeff Campbell's Clean Team: Speed Cleaning Rules and More

and how to maintain machines and the like so they don't wear out. For instance, Campbell notes that overstuffing a washing machine will take years off its life. Instead of breaking the washer, do two loads. Never thought of that.

FlyLady.net
www.flylady.net

Maria Cilley, a "sidetracked home executive," is the "FlyLady." Cilley offers a whole year-full of ideas about how to quickly organize and maintain the home—along with suggestions for getting a little exercise. Her basic message is that we all need to get on top of the chaos in our lives so that we can love ourselves. Sign up for daily emails that walk subscribers through "baby steps" toward control over their clutter and, ultimately, their lives. Watch her videos and listen to her podcasts, too.

MarthaStewart.com: Home & Garden

www.marthastewart.com/home-decorating

Explore the menu on the left side of the page. See the entries marked "Home Improvement & Repairs" and "Homekeeping Solutions." Here is where Martha hides solid cleaning and repair tips to keep the house in top shape.

About.com: Housekeeping

housekeeping.about.com

Former teacher Sarah Aguirre now turns her professional skills to running a home filled with four children. She presents a variety of articles on cleaning tips and techniques (including keeping daily, weekly, and monthly cleaning schedules in a notebook: ugh!), advice on making organic cleaning products, and reviews of soaps and tools. Aguirre is so thorough that she even details steps for hand-washing dishes.

Estimators and Calculators

How much material will you need to complete a project? And how much is it going to cost? Use these online tools to get a good idea.

ServiceMagic: Project Tools

www.servicemagic.com/resources.tools.html

Got a project or enhancement in mind? Use these estimators, calculators, visualizers, and planners to get an idea of what your improvement will look like and how much money you will need.

Lowe's: Project Calculators

www.lowes.com/cd_Project+Calculator_905619130_

Lowe's has collected 18 online calculators to help with your home improvement projects. See how much carpet, blown insulation, or even rafter length you need.

Ace Paint Estimator

services.acehardware.com/paint

Find out how much paint you have to buy to cover the walls in a room or on a house. Just enter your measurements to get the results.

Concrete.com: Concrete Materials Calculators

www.concrete.com/calculators/concrete-materials-calculators

Use these three calculators (concrete volume, block wall, or concrete column) to figure how much concrete you need for a project.

Home Improvement Apps

Can smart phone programs help you fix your house? Why not! Here are a couple of them designed for the iPhone.

iTunes: iHandy Carpenter

itunes.apple.com/app/ihandy-carpenter/id293621500?mt=8

This $2 iTunes app turns your iPhone into a level, a plumb bob, a protractor, and a ruler. Put them all together, and they become a clinometer. Yes, you can use your phone to measure tilt.

iTunes: HandyMan Sidekick

itunes.apple.com/app/handyman-sidekick/id301884224?mt=8

Two bucks buys this iPhone app that helps calculate how much of any building material you will need to buy to complete a project. It's a flashlight, too.

Can't (or Shouldn't) Do It Yourself?

When the job is just too big, as our collapsed cesspool line was, or if you mess up your home repair, as I did when I installed the new bathroom faucet, it is time to call a professional. Here are some services to hook you up with skilled labor.

Contractors.com

www.contractors.com

Search Contractors.com's database by keyword, company, or area of expertise. Also, rate your contractor and see others' ratings. Read articles on techniques about how to choose a quality professional for your project.

Handyman Online

www.handymanonline.com

Use this site to find local certified service professionals ready to do your job. There is even a live chat feature on the site to help searchers who don't know how to begin.

ImproveNet

www.improvenet.com

Use ImproveNet to find a contractor for really big jobs. Describe the parameters of your project and ImproveNet will scour its database of nearly 30,000 professionals to find a contractor to fit your needs.

Angie's List

www.angieslist.com

No search for services would be complete without consulting Angie's List. Founded by Ohioan Angie Hicks in 1995, this service maintains a database of home service providers (plumbers, painters, contractors, etc.) and collects reviews from members on their performance. Angie's List charges a fee for membership:

$4.50 per month on a per month basis, or less than $18 for a full year subscription. This keeps reviews honest and personal.

Back to Normal

Things are happy again at our house. Now we can do the wash, clean the dishes, and flush the toilet all on the same day. Sheesh. That seems like a lot of work just to get back to normal. But that's home ownership for you!

10

Applications:
Finding a Job Using the Internet

The news tells the sad story: The last recession left behind a discouragingly high unemployment rate. Unemployment is a "lagging indicator," so even when the economy improves, hiring doesn't occur for a while.

The web can help. For one thing, it makes it easy to search job listings, as most classified ads are now hosted online. Not only that, but we can post our resumes on the web where employers can easily find them.

The web offers free ways to sharpen our job skills with lessons for using word processing and spreadsheet programs and even for learning Spanish. It hosts free resume and cover letter generators.

Finally, we can get in touch with old friends and colleagues using social networking sites like Facebook and LinkedIn. We can then enlist our web of friends to help us connect with employment opportunities.

The First Step

Most people start a job search by scanning the classified ads. Online classifieds are almost as old as the web, having been around for about 15 years. By now, there are so many employment websites, it often seems like they might outnumber the actual jobs available. Therefore, it is most efficient to search blocks of them at once with employment metasearch engines. It may also help to slap a resume on a website where employers might find it.

Simply Hired
www.simplyhired.com

In return for free registration, use this job search engine to scour the web for classifieds in the U.S., the U.K., Australia, or India. Simply Hired also offers statistics about salaries, city demographics, and hiring trends. Search for known job titles or browse listings by industry, category, or location. A "Special Search" looks for jobs friendly to moms, seniors, and dog lovers, among other categories. Use the site's widgets to track job announcements on iGoogle, blogs, MySpace, Facebook, and on mobile phones.

Indeed
www.indeed.com

Create a free account to search and capture jobs collated from all the major job boards, professional associations, newspapers, and the employment pages of major corporations. Search for employment by job title or browse by employment categories or cities. See hiring trends for specific jobs, and join in discussions about them. Indeed also has sites for Canada, the U.K., France, Germany, Spain, and India.

Jobfox
www.jobfox.com

This site is like eHarmony for employment. Jobfox asks applicants to fill out an in-depth profile. It uses the answers to match job seekers with employment opportunities, so it's a prescreened match.

Indeed

RealMatch

www.realmatch.com

On RealMatch, you play the coy damsel-in-waiting. Fill in the title of the job you want, enter your search radius, and upload your resume, all for free. Now you wait for anonymous evaluations by prospective employers. It's like Jobfox, but without the compatibility matching. Another difference: You can block yourself from being searched by your current employer.

oDesk

www.odesk.com

oDesk is a "freelance liaison" firm, meaning that it not only lets freelancers from around the world post their portfolios for employers to find, but it also manages money. Employers put payments in an escrow account at oDesk. The money is released to the freelancer upon job completion. Other sites for finding freelance work include Elance (www.elance.com) and Guru.com (www.guru.com).

Mashable: Career Toolbox—100+ Places to Find Jobs
mashable.com/2008/12/16/find-jobs

Don't trust metasearch and can't wait around to be discovered? Start plowing through this massive collection of employment sites, roughly categorized by industry or applicant type. There are international job search sites listed here, too.

craigslist
www.craigslist.org

Never neglect to peruse the classifieds on craigslist. There may be jewels among the freely posted dross. As these are not paid ads, they won't show up on the metasearch sites.

Advice

When starting a job hunt, let the experts help you brush up your resume and thank-you card writing skills. Here are some tried-and-true job-seeking advice portals.

JobHuntersBible.com
www.jobhuntersbible.com

He's a preacher. He's a career counselor. He's a warm washcloth over the eyes of the desperately unemployed. Dick Bolles is the author of the best-selling job-hunting book, *What Color Is Your Parachute?* This site supplements that volume. As always, Bolles encourages a thorough technique: to understand oneself and what one wants out of life before running off and blindly applying for a job. On this note, he offers links to self-assessment sites and advice about how to use them. Bolles underscores the need to research employers and make personal connections in the job search. This approach, Bolles asserts, will lead not only to new jobs, but personal satisfaction and growth.

The Riley Guide: Employment Opportunities and Job Resources on the Internet
www.rileyguide.com

Librarian and author Margaret F. Dikel (formerly Margaret F. Riley) compiled and maintains this comprehensive job search portal. Dikel starts off with preparation, the hardest part of any job hunt. She also offers coping links for those who've lost their jobs. Self-assessment approaches are here, too, along with access to training, certification, and internship resources. Dikel also links to resume advice, company research, salary guides, and most importantly, job listings of every sort.

JobStar: California Job Search Guide
jobstar.org

Job seekers in California should instantly point their browser to librarian Mary-Ellen Mort's JobStar. Mort understands that most people do not want to have to move when they take a new job. So, she provides employment resources clustered by region. Search local resources in Los Angeles, San Diego, San Francisco, and Sacramento. Users anywhere will profit from a visit to JobStar Central for advice about resumes, hidden jobs, and salary information.

Social Networking for Jobs

We can search through the classifieds and sometimes get lucky. Still, the word on the street is overwhelming: It's not what you know, it's who you know. The big new story of job searching lies with social networking sites, specifically the triumvirate of LinkedIn, Twitter, and Facebook. As new users flock to these sites, they are now reaching the critical mass that makes them useful as job resources.

Connections on the social networking sites can be the ticket to finding a job in this stinky economy. But a network doesn't happen overnight. Sign up on all three of these now and start hooking up with old friends. Then, if the time ever comes when you need them, they'll be in place.

LinkedIn

www.linkedin.com

Play "Six Degrees of Separation" to land a job! Join LinkedIn for free and then post your resume. Then, invite everyone you know (who is already a member) to join your network. Search through ready-made lists of classmates and colleagues. Scour your web-based email contacts for network-bait. Then, look for jobs. LinkedIn will tell you who knows whom in your network that might give you an inside edge.

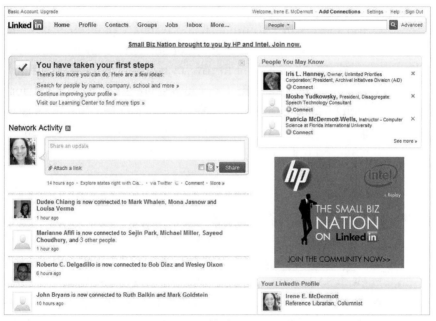

LinkedIn

Twitter

twitter.com

A free Twitter account lets users "microblog," that is, publish short (maximum of 140 characters) advice, aphorisms, and status updates (known as "Tweets") to others who have subscribed to their feed. It is considered polite to reciprocate by following others' feeds. The result should be an ever-changing stream of news flowing between you and those in your network. The application has shown promise as a kind of emergency broadcast system, as subscribers can send and receive updates from mobile phones. The flow of news should allow users to broadcast the need for a job and receive quick responses from friends.

Facebook
www.facebook.com

Facebook is an ideal way to establish and maintain an effective business network. If I needed a job, I'm sure that one of my newly found old friends would jump in to help. These folks are spread all over the country. Surely one of them would know someone who is hiring and could get me an interview. A free Facebook app is available for all smart phones.

Mashable: 7 Secrets to Getting Your Next Job Using Social Media
mashable.com/2009/01/05/job-search-secrets/?cp=1

Author Dan Schawbel schools us on exactly how to use Twitter, LinkedIn, and Facebook to sell our "brand" and connect to real people within companies. He finishes off by advising job seekers to make videos of themselves for uploading to YouTube.

Mashable: How To—Build the Ultimate Social Media Resume
mashable.com/2009/01/13/social-media-resume

Schawbel advises seekers of technology jobs or other advanced positions to set up blogs and websites to attract potential employers.

Resume and Cover Letter Generators

What good is having a place to store a resume and cover letter if you are not sure how to write one in the first place? Never fear. Here are some free online generators that offer the proper framework for these documents. Type in your relevant information and the programs generate the finished products in the proper format.

CareerZone: Write Your Resume
www.nycareerzone.org/cz/resources/jobseeker/resume.jsp

For job seekers who don't want to struggle with layouts, the New York State Department of Labor has prepared this online resume generator. Users simply fill in the online form with relevant information: education, experience, and abilities. The program allows users to export their resumes in HTML format, in Microsoft Word as a rich text format (RTF) file, or into Adobe Acrobat's PDF.

Teachnology: Professional Teacher Resume Maker
www.teach-nology.com/web_tools/resume

Although designed for educators, you can easily adapt this resume generator from Teachnology for almost any position. The site also offers a cover letter generator (www.teach-nology.com/web_tools/cover_letter). Get a well-organized cover letter simply by filling in the blanks.

NIEFS Cover Letter Work Sheet
www.niefs.net/resumes/coverletter.htm

The North Island Employment Foundations Society (NIEFS) of Campbell River in British Columbia hosts this cover letter generator that features helpful hints about what type of information to enter in each slot.

Learning Microsoft Word

Microsoft Word is the word processing standard in the workplace. Even open source programs resemble it and work in a similar way. You can use these tutorials to gain word processing and other business software competencies.

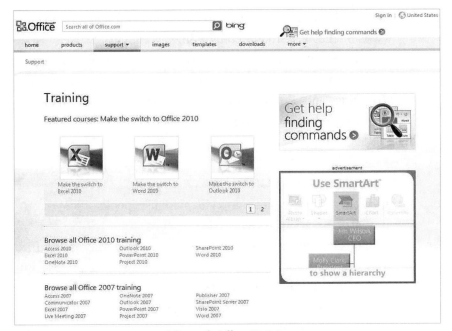

Microsoft Office: Training

Microsoft Office: Training

office.microsoft.com/en-us/training/default.aspx

Microsoft itself now offers free online tutorials about how to use all its Office products, including Word, Excel, Outlook, and even OneNote. Learn older versions of the software as well as the new Office 2010 products.

Baycon Group: Microsoft Word 2007 Tutorial

www.baycongroup.com/wlesson0.htm

Denise Etheridge wrote this series of clear, methodical lessons about how to use Microsoft Word. She starts from the beginning, giving an overview of what the software is designed to do. She addresses issues that novice users often face, including "Understanding Non-Printing Characters." Baycon Group maintains other tutorials on this site, too, including ones for Windows Vista, PowerPoint, and even Adobe Flash.

Internet4Classrooms: Word Tutorials and Information

www.internet4classrooms.com/on-line_word.htm

Susan Brooks and Bill Byles have written these tutorials to help teachers become proficient with technology. Lessons include "Inserting and Editing Images in MS Word," "Designing a Newsletter Using Microsoft Word," and my favorite, "Part of a Border Won't Print?"

Essential Microsoft Office 2007

www.educationworld.com/a_tech/columnists/poole/office_tutorials/Lesson1_2007.pdf

In this chapter from his online book Essential Microsoft Office 2007: Tutorials for Teachers, Bernie Poole, associate professor of education and instructional technology at the University of Pittsburgh at Johnstown, Pennsylvania, offers instructions about how to use Word 2007. Download other chapters of his book here, too, including "Intro to Access" and the all-important "Mail Merge." Requires the free Adobe Acrobat Reader (get.adobe.com/reader).

Learning Microsoft Excel

The spreadsheet is useful for so many things. Knowing how to use one is an essential competency for many businesses. Get up-to-speed with these online tutorials.

St. Mary's County Library: Microsoft Excel Classes

www.stmalib.org/compvids.html

St. Mary's County Library in Maryland offers this series of six tutorials to help learn how to use Microsoft's Excel 2007. Download the handouts here, too.

YouTube: MotionTraining Microsoft Excel Tutorials

www.youtube.com/watch?v=8L1OVkw2ZQ8

U.K.-based MotionTraining offers a whole channel of 17 excellent Microsoft Excel tutorials absolutely free. This is the first one. A very pleasant way to learn or hone a valuable skill.

YouTube: ExcellsFun Excel Basics #1

www.youtube.com/watch?v=XmSp2-Fa4rg

Mike Gel Girvin, business instructor at Highline Community College in Des Moines, Washington, delves into the mathematical functions available from Excel in this series of Flash videos on YouTube. He links to accompanying instructional workbooks that you can download from his site (flightline.highline.edu/mgirvin/excelisfun.htm).

Learning Microsoft Outlook

Outlook is the ubiquitous email program used by business. Love it or hate it, we all must learn to use it. Here's help.

Learn the Net: Step-by-Step: Sending E-Mail Attachments

www.learnthenet.com/how-to/attach-files-to-email/index.php

People aren't born knowing how to attach a file to an email. This lesson clearly explains a skill essential in today's business settings.

Productivity Portfolio: Outlook

www.timeatlas.com/mos/Email/Outlook

Take advantage of all Outlook has to offer, including calendars, tasks, and notes, with these tutorials from Northern California's Anne Hennegar. Tips include "Building Outlook Distribution Lists," "Recurring vs. Regenerated Tasks," and "Staying Current with Contacts."

TechRepublic: Microsoft Outlook

search.techrepublic.com.com/search/microsoft+outlook.html

For more advanced users, TechRepublic offers articles that show how to get the most out of Outlook. Tips include how to re-send a message, how to store sent mail so that it can be easily searched, and how to get around the printing bugs in Outlook 2007.

How-To Geek: Microsoft Outlook

www.howtogeek.com/tag/microsoft-office/#outlook

A computer programmer frustrated with the quality of free computer advice on the web started writing his own back in 2006. The result is this site. Check out his articles about Microsoft Outlook for insights about how to wrangle it better.

Learning Spanish

A recent survey from the U.S. Census Bureau reports that in five states, one in five people are native Spanish speakers. For some jobs, it is not only wise to know Spanish, it's a requirement. Use these free resources to start speaking Spanish today!

StudySpanish.com

www.studyspanish.com

Users can register for free to take tests and register grades on this handsome site, which offers beginning, intermediate, and advanced lessons. The site also offers a "premium" package for $165, which includes a course on CD called *Camino del éxito* (Path to Success) along with audio podcasts.

iTunesU

www.apple.com/itunes

Download iTunes for free to gain access to university courses via iTunesU. Listen to podcasts about a variety of issues in Spanish culture and society in Portales: Beginner's Spanish from Open University. The Five Colleges of Ohio provides free Conversations in Spanish. For fun, listen to Coffee Break Spanish, short practical lessons in conversational Spanish taught by the Radio Lingua Network.

Livemocha

www.livemocha.com

Seattle-based Livemocha offers heavily graphical language courses in return for free registration, along with the opportunity to pair up with native speakers online. For $25, "premium" users also get tutoring and podcasts.

Writing Tips

Writing clearly and concisely is a basic workplace competency. These sites offer advice about writing workplace communications.

Purdue Online Writing Lab: Writing the Basic Business Letter

owl.english.purdue.edu/owl/resource/653/01

The Purdue Online Writing Lab offers more than 200 articles with tips for academic and business writing, including this collection describing how to write a business letter. Find sample letters here that illustrate the proper format.

Grammarphobia.com: Test Your Email IQ

www.grammarphobia.com/email.html

Patricia T. O'Conner and Stewart Kellerman offer sensible tips for business email such as making sure to include a subject line, keeping the note short, and checking the spelling and grammar!

Telephone Etiquette

Any service sector job will involve giving good customer service, often over the phone. These sites can help brush up public service skills.

Phone Pro: Customer Service and Telephone Etiquette

www.phonepro.org

Phone Pro's call center trainers wrote this collection of articles with insights for giving good customer service over the phone. We could all use some of that advice!

The Phone Coach: Phone Skills and Telephone Etiquette Articles
www.thephonecoach.com/PhoneEtiquetteArticles.htm

Improve your all-important phone skills with these articles from The Phone Coach. Articles include "Using the Proper Tone of Voice" and "The Importance of Creating a Great First Impression."

WorkEtiquette: Telephone Etiquette at Work
www.worketiquette.co.uk/telephone-etiquette-at-work.html

Britain's WorkEtiquette presents tips for good work telephone practices including answering quickly and being prepared, as well as "Speak slightly more slowly on the phone than you would if you were having a general face-to-face conversation."

Let's Get to Work!

The employment landscape may have been permanently altered by the recent recession. Still, I hope that these web-based tools will help anyone who wants a job to find one … the sooner the better!

11

Hard Drive:
Buying and Repairing Automobiles

"I just spent $2,000 on my old car, and it still has an oil leak!" my colleague Lynda declared. She was driving a 1993 Chrysler Eagle Vision that was starting to require almost constant maintenance. "I knew that my tires were bald and that the bushings were going out on my rack-and-pinion steering," she recounted. Then, as she drove around a corner, the front wheels started clicking.

"I had a 'deer in the headlights' moment," she recalls. "Should I sell my car or fix it?" Lynda took a deep breath and handed over the $800 for tie rods, two tires, and new bushings. Three days later, her car overheated. She pulled into a gas station with smoke billowing from under the hood and coolant spurting out of the bottom of the vehicle. "The gas station attendant yelled at me for getting anti-freeze on his pavement," she mused. Lynda had the car towed to her mechanic, where the fix for the overheat came in at $1,100. "Apparently, it needed an expensive part," she sighed. "And the oil still leaks. Now I own an old car with an oil leak, no air conditioning, and a bump shift in a rebuilt transmission."

What's a gal to do? We live in Los Angeles where a running car is a must. Should Lynda buy a replacement car? How can she perform a cost/benefit analysis of her situation? The web hosts sites that can help with the decision of whether to repair an old car or buy another.

About.com: How Much Is Enough?

autorepair.about.com/od/autorepair12/a/aa020301a.htm

Vincent Ciulla advises readers on when to repair an old car and when to let it go. He recommends a professional vehicle inspection. Of course, sometimes, you can't afford the repair or another car. "Get as much information on the shape your car is in and you can make a more informed decision," Ciulla says.

General Automotive Repair

Get an idea of what is wrong with your car and how much it will cost to fix it with these sites.

AutoMD

www.automd.com

Use the Diagnose option and consider your car's symptoms: What do you hear, smell, feel, or see? Or is the problem simply, "Ugh! It won't start!" Click through the decision tree to see what might be wrong with your vehicle. Then use AutoMD to get an estimate on repairs and to find a reliable shop. Or browse its library of articles and videos about how to fix it yourself.

RepairPal

repairpal.com

Find local mechanics and get estimates of what repairs should cost for newer, popular cars based on your location. Register your car and keep its maintenance records here. Browse articles and forums about auto repair. Download the free app to your iPhone to find local repair shops (itunes.apple.com/app/repairpal-auto-repair-expert/id300996215?mt=8) or just find the mobile site with your phone's browser (m.repairpal.com).

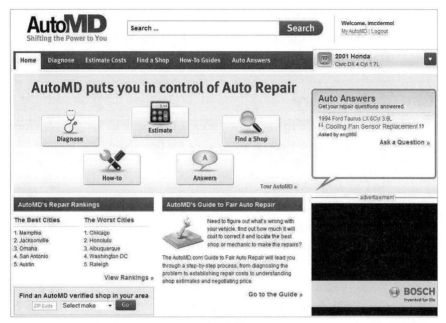

AutoMD

DriverSide

www.driverside.com

"Manage" your car's life by registering it with DriverSide. Receive recall alerts, find local mechanics, and learn the current value of your vehicle in case you want to sell it.

About.com: Auto Repair

autorepair.about.com

Maybe you just don't have the money for extensive repairs or another car. Matthew Wright of the About.com Auto Repair Guide promotes "automotive empowerment," that is, learning about your car so you can either fix it yourself or understand what repairs are necessary to save money and avoid "upselling." Wright explains life lessons that you should have learned from your dad: how to check the oil and tire pressure and do other routine maintenance. He offers simple fixes that can save money and aggravation, like tightening a muffler bolt or replacing a broken exhaust hanger. He gets into hairier projects, too, such as changing your own fuel tank and replacing a brake line.

Car Maintenance

Regular vehicle maintenance goes a long way to keep a car from needing repairs. Browse these sites for tips about how to do it.

Be Car Care Aware

www.carcare.org

The Automotive Aftermarket Industry Association offers general advice about how to maintain a car and even how to prepare it for summer or winter driving.

Car Talk: Actual Car Information

cartalk.com/menus/info.html#owning

Radio personalities Tom and Ray Magliozzi know how to make car care entertaining. Read their advice here.

Michelin: Tire Care & Buying Guide

www.michelinman.com/tire-care

Got a problem with your tires? The Michelin Man offers a Tire Diagnosis tool to keep you rolling. Find the best way to lengthen the life of your tires and what to look for when you need to buy new ones. Learn to read a sidewall and understand why the "penny test" is important. ("If the tread is worn below 2/32 of an inch, water can't be channeled away from the tread. This can cause hydroplaning at high speeds." Yikes!)

Wise Bread: Remove Car Dents Quickly and Cheaply

www.wisebread.com/remove-car-dents-quickly-and-cheaply

Colorado adman Paul Michael offers three video links that show how to get dents out of cars using inexpensive materials. The first video shows a technique using dry ice. The second and third

demonstrate the miraculous power of a hair dryer or a lighter followed by an icy blast of compressed air on metal car skin. Pop! It's
enough to put body shops out of business.

On-Board Diagnostics

Any car made since 1996 carries a computer that records when
something goes wrong. When it detects a problem, it turns on the
dashboard "check engine" light. Mechanics find out what the light
means by reaching under the dash and plugging in a code reader, a
device that retrieves the on-board diagnostics. Laypeople can also
buy code readers for $60 or more to read the computer's mind.
(Lynda's car was built in 1993, before the OBD code computers
became standard, so this would not help her.)

OBD-II Trouble Codes

www.obd-codes.com/trouble_codes

Translate your OBD-II code (for cars built in 1996 and later)
into English here. Many OBD-I codes from the late 1980s to early
1990s can be found here: autorepair.about.com/od/obdcodedata
base/The_Exhaustive_Database_of_OBDI_and_OBDII_Engine_
Codes.htm.

AutoZone: In Store Services

www.autozone.com/autozone/inourstores/services.jsp#Testing

Don't want to drop a bunch of dough on an OBD code reader?
Drop by any AutoZone store and have your codes checked for free.
AutoZone also lends specialty tools for auto repair.

Manuals

The manual that comes with your car can answer lots of questions
about how to troubleshoot common problems. Third-party repair
manuals can also help. If you can't find them through your public
library, you can buy the manuals through these sources.

Haynes Repair Manuals

www.haynes.com

Haynes is among the leading publishers of car repair manuals, offering detailed instructions for the do-it-yourselfer. Search this site to buy manuals specific to your vehicle. Browse Haynes' free video podcasts for quick car maintenance tutorials on how to replace a spark plug or change transmission fluid (www.haynes.com/video.downloads).

ALLDATAdiy.com

www.alldatadiy.com

This site from AutoZone is geared mainly toward professional mechanics who want to buy repair information. Still, ALLDATA does offer some help for do-it-yourselfers. Browse featured tech articles written by ASE-certified master technicians and engine machinists (www.alldatadiy.com/techtips/index.html). For about $25 per year, you can buy a subscription to ALLDATA's database of repair and diagnostic data covering more than 20,000 vehicles dating back to 1982.

Evaluating and Pricing Cars

If Lynda decides to donate her clunker and buy a new or used car, she'll have no trouble finding help deciding on a purchase. Here are some new and used car evaluation sites.

How Stuff Works: Consumer Guide Automotive

consumerguideauto.howstuffworks.com

Consumer Guide, rival to the better known Consumer Reports, offers this overview covering all aspects of buying a car. Find reviews of new and used cars and get the scoop about upcoming models. Follow links to financing services, warranty, and insurance information.

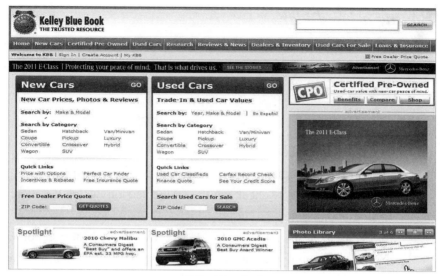

Kelley Blue Book

Kelley Blue Book

kbb.com

Since 1926, Kelley Blue Book has been the de facto barometer of a car's worth. The online version is so much simpler to use than the book. Kelley Blue Book offers excellent tools for comparing new cars, too.

Edmunds.com

www.edmunds.com

Here is the thinking person's guide to new and used automobiles. Evaluation of used car values generally run lower and perhaps more realistically than those offered on the Kelley Blue Book site. Try the True Cost to Own tool to see what the car will really cost over time.

TrueCar

www.truecar.com

What is a good price for a new car? Find out what your dealer paid, what a fair price would be for you, and what you should never pay for the new car of your dreams.

Buying a Used Car

A used car may be a good bargain if it has been well maintained and is fairly new. But how to find a reliable used car? These websites can help.

AutoTrader

www.autotrader.com

You see the print version of this publication at your local convenience store. Now check out the online version, which has more than 1,900,000 new and used vehicles available for search. Many of the used car listings offer free CARFAX vehicle history reports. You can also sell your own car through AutoTrader in return for a listing fee.

Enterprise Car Sales

www.enterprisecarsales.com

One strategy for finding a reliable used car is to purchase a lightly used one from an established rental company. These companies turn over their inventory often, so many of the cars they sell have fewer than 20,000 miles on them and still qualify for a new car warranty. You can buy these nearly new cars for about one-third less than the new car price. Enterprise Car Sales lists its nationwide, late-model, certified used cars online. Just type in your ZIP code to see cars available within about a 100-mile radius.

Hertz Car Sales

www.hertzcarsales.com

Hertz offers low fixed prices on its well-maintained vehicles, which eliminates the haggling factor. Search its inventory by location and/or vehicle type. Hertz also offers a Rent2Buy program (www.hertzrent2buy.com) in which the potential buyer drives the used car for a few days as a rental. If you like it, then you can buy it.

Enterprise Car Sales

Auto Loans

Car dealers are happy to offer financing for their new cars. Still, you can often get a better deal through an independent lender. Visit these sites to research auto loans.

Bankrate.com: Auto

www.bankrate.com/auto.aspx

Visit Bankrate.com for comprehensive, objective information about current loan rates, as well as links to online lenders. Use the site's financial calculators and read advice on how to make the best deal on a loan before you even visit an auto dealer.

LendingTree Autos

www.lendingtree.com/auto-loans

Enter your request at LendingTree, and it will return up to four bids for your loan. Use its on-site tools to compare cars, get quotes, and even shop for used cars. Read advice about saving money on car loans here, too.

Auto Insurance

If you buy a new car, you might want to reevaluate your car insurance. Shop around for the best deals with these independent sites.

InsWeb

www.insweb.com

Visit this insurance rate comparison site and click on Auto Insurance to request quotes from reliable auto insurance companies in your area. Read articles about how to save money on insurance here, too.

Insurance.com

www.insurance.com

Thirteen car insurance companies compete to offer you the best rates through this insurance comparison site.

Sell or Fix?

In the end, the unreliability of the 1993 Chrysler Eagle Vision proved overwhelming. So Lynda bought a new Chrysler Sebring.

You can do all the research on the web you want, but sometimes brand loyalty beats everything.

Part four

Amusements

All work and no play makes Jack a dull boy! Our passions give meaning to life, and the web has plenty of information about them, no matter what they are. Here, I cover some of the big things we do for fun: traveling, playing with the dog, and growing our own food and then cooking it exquisitely. Enjoy!

12

Virtual Vegetables:
Websites for Growing and Preserving Food

Aunt Bert, now in her late 80s, scrapes a dab of dinner onto some tin foil, wraps it up, and tucks it in the freezer. She has no money worries. Still, as a child of the Depression, she will not waste a scrap of food even today. The Depression was not just a hard time; it was brain damage.

In the 1930s and then during World War II, food shortages in the U.S. were a way of life. The government urged citizens to fight back by growing their own "victory gardens." According to the USDA Cooperative State Research, Education and Extension Service (CSREES; www.csrees.usda.gov/qlinks/extension.html), "In 1943 some 20 million victory gardens produced more than 40 percent of the vegetables grown for that year's fresh consumption." Forty percent! This remarkable public effort helped to unite the nation and win the war.

Now as then, our nation faces troubles at home and abroad. Would it help to battle these problems in our own yards with hoes and rakes? Growing some of our own food would help us to feel more self-sufficient and save money. Because our produce would not have to travel thousands of miles to get to us, our gardens would work against climate change. Our bodies would get sun and exercise. And we would enjoy the health benefits of eating fresh vegetables and fruit.

Garden Gates

Growing tomatoes improves my health and also saves the world? I'll do it! But how do I start? Wouldn't you know it: The web overflows with bounteous advice about how to grow food in the family garden. Here are some gardening overviews.

National Gardening Association: Food Gardening Guide

www.garden.org/foodguide/browse

"Whether you're growing basil, blueberries, or bok choy, the Food Gardening Guide will give you all the information you need to succeed." New and experienced gardeners can start at this site to find advice about planting, fertilizing, and pests.

The Victory Garden

www.pbs.org/wgbh/victorygarden

Landscape architect Jamie Durie hosts *The Victory Garden*, TV's longest-running garden show. The accompanying website offers advice on growing food in a kitchen garden. Read and watch videos about great new varieties of vegetables as well as garden project ideas and maintenance tips. The Victory Garden can be downloaded as a podcast.

About.com: Gardening

gardening.about.com

Marie Iannotti offers general gardening advice in a blog-like format. That is, her main page offers timely, newly written short articles. Subject categories in the sidebar link to pieces about a variety of garden topics, including "Choosing Plants" and "Gardening with Kids." There are videos here, too.

National Gardening Association: Food Gardening Guide

Urban and Small Space Gardening

We don't all live on large plots of land that lend themselves to a generous kitchen garden. Turns out, that is no barrier to home horticulture. Visit these sites to learn about container and small space gardening.

Victory Gardens

www.sfvictorygardens.org

In 2008, the city of San Francisco made it a priority to help its citizens to grow food wherever they could. To that end, the city put up this site with very specific instructions on how to build a successful raised bed in a small, urban garden.

Sunset: How to Grow Veggies in Pots

www.sunset.com/garden/fruits-veggies/how-to-grow-veggies-in-pots-00400000012149

Sunset Magazine's Lauren Bonar Swezey shows us how to choose the best containers, find the right spot, and pick the best vegetables for successful harvests grown in pots.

Virginia Cooperative Extension:
Vegetable Gardening in Containers

www.ext.vt.edu/pubs/envirohort/426-336/426-336.html

Diane Relf wrote this instruction sheet for the Virginia Cooperative Extension in which she details exactly how to grow food in containers. "Vegetables grown for their fruits generally need at least five hours of full, direct sunlight each day," she cautions, although she concedes that the requirement can be fudged by placing reflective materials around the plants.

EarthTainer

earthtainer.tomatofest.com

Use these instructions to make a self-watering container using Rubbermaid tubs. Or buy an EarthBox (earthbox.com) or an Organic Tomato Success Kit from the Gardner's Supply Company (www.gardeners.com; search for *tomato success*).

Gardening Blogs

Backyard and rooftop gardeners burn with passion for their pastime. Their enthusiasm finds voice on blogs. Experience their love and maybe get some good advice in the bargain.

Urban Homestead

urbanhomestead.org

Talk about your extreme self-sufficiency! Since 2001, Jules Dervaes and his family have been growing almost all their own food (including chickens for eggs and goats for milk—they are vegetarian) and have even been making their own biodiesel fuel in their modest backyard near Los Angeles. Pick up a little of their defiant mojo by touching their blog.

You Grow Girl

www.yougrowgirl.com

Writer Gayla Trail has been blogging about home gardening for over a decade. Explore her site by category to read her funny yet insightful musings on home gardening dilemmas and discoveries.

Cold Climate Gardening: Hardy Plants for Hardy Souls

www.coldclimategardening.com

In upstate New York, Kathy Purdy, mother of 12, writes about gardening where winters are long, dark, and deeply frozen (as in, -30 degrees Fahrenheit). This woman can get potatoes from permafrost.

Composting

Can "smug" be a compost catalyst? Because I get a squiggle of self-satisfaction every evening when I tap my used coffee grounds into my kitchen compost pail, knowing that they will wind up in my backyard bin along with bread heels, egg shells, fallen fruit, and even shredded bank statements. In the spring, I slide up the panel at the base of the compost bin, and out pours black gold, made from a year's worth of garbage, ready to mix with my potting soil.

CalRecycle: Home Composting

www.calrecycle.ca.gov/Organics/HomeCompost

The State of California walks you through the basics of composting at home.

**You Grow Girl: Things You Can Compost
That You Didn't Think You Could**

www.yougrowgirl.com/thedirt/2008/11/17/things-
you-can-compost-that-you-didnt-think-you-could

Gayla Trail cuts down on trash day and helps her garden by composting her hair, garden dust, bad wine, and even gum!

Cornell Composting: Worm Composting Basics

compost.css.cornell.edu/worms/basics.html

Worm poop makes great compost! Here's how to make a vermicomposter out of newspaper and a plastic bin. Add worms and vegetable scraps, and you're set.

Soil

Gardening is like house painting. It's all prep. Here's how to fix your dirt so it is healthy and ready to support your veggies.

The Victory Garden: Soil 101

www.pbs.org/wgbh/victorygarden/grow/primers_projects/soil.html

Here is a primer on getting your garden soil ready to rock, courtesy of PBS's long-running television garden show.

UMass: Soil and Plant Tissue Testing Laboratory

www.umass.edu/plsoils/soiltest

Score a basic soil test for $9 from the University of Massachusetts Amherst Extension. Put dirt in a zip-top bag, send it through the mail, and get analysis and guidance about what you need to make your garden explode with vegetable goodness.

Frost

The climate may be changing, but we still have winter. Gardeners in intemperate climes must know their planting "zone" and the projected date of the last frost to take full advantage of their abbreviated growing seasons. When is it safe for you to plant? Find out with these sites.

National Gardening Association: USDA Hardiness Zone Finder

www.garden.org/zipzone

The U.S. Department of Agriculture (USDA) has divided the country into 11 zones, which represent differences of 10 degrees Fahrenheit in the lowest winter temperature. Enter your ZIP code at this site to find out when you can safely plant your veggies.

NESDIS: Freeze/Frost Data

cdo.ncdc.noaa.gov/cgi-bin/climatenormals/climatenormals.pl

Click on "Frost/Freeze Data 1971–2001" to use the widget from the National Environmental Satellite, Data and Information Service (NESDIS), which will find station freeze/frost probability tables for your state.

USDA: Cooperative Extension System Offices

www.csrees.usda.gov/Extension/index.html

If you need more detailed technical help with garden questions, you can always find it at your local USDA-CSREES. "These offices are staffed by one or more experts who provide useful, practical, and research-based information to agricultural producers, small business owners, youth, consumers, and others in rural areas and communities of all sizes." Find your nearest office by visiting this page.

Water

In my semi-arid climate of Southern California, vegetable plants must be watered every day. Almost all of our water is imported either from Northern California or the Colorado River (not counting the Perrier), so it is very important to use as little as possible. Here are some tips on using our precious water resource wisely.

Southern Nevada Water Authority: Drip Watering Tips

www.snwa.com/html/land_irrig_drip.html

Who knows more about saving water than farmers in the deserts of southern Nevada? Get tips for getting the most out of precious imported liquid from this Southern Nevada Water Authority site.

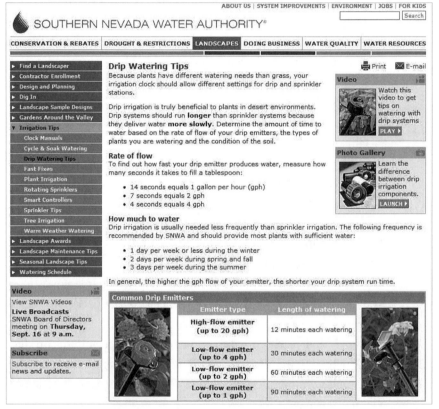

Southern Nevada Water Authority: Drip Watering Tips

LA Times: No Reason to Dig Any Deeper

articles.latimes.com/2008/jun/12/home/hm-nodig12

In this article from June 2008, Lisa Boone profiles Pat Marfisi, who has mastered the Australian art of growing vegetables on a lasagna of alfalfa, straw, and compost, with a schmear of bone meal in between. He hardly ever has to water his plants. His exact method is explained here: www.latimes.com/features/home/la-hm-nodigside12-2008jun12,0,3026262.story.

LA Times: Follow-Up to No Reason to Dig Any Deeper
www.latimes.com/features/home/la-hm-sequels28-2009mar28, 0,3890846.story

Boone updates the previous story with tips for how to keep the Australian method working in the second year.

Seeds

Now that we've got our infrastructure in place, what shall we plant? The neighborhood nursery sells normal plants and seeds. Still, if we want to branch out, we can order rare and heirloom vegetable seeds from these sites.

Seeds of Change
www.seedsofchange.com

This company makes a point of conserving heirloom seeds in sufficient quantity to sell in retail outlets. Discover delicious vegetable variety and preserve biodiversity all at the same time!

Victory Seeds
www.victoryseeds.com

Oregon's Victory Seeds is a small, family-owned company that also sells rare, open-pollinated, and heirloom garden seeds.

Botanical Interests
www.botanicalinterests.com

This family business run from Colorado features beautiful illustrations that will inspire the vegetable and herb gardener. Find helpful gardening tips here, too. Botanical Interests also offers a highly-rated $6 iTunes app (itunes.apple.com/us/app/botanical-interests/id331905040?mt=8). This beautifully designed electronic

Botanical Interests

primer tells what, where, and when to plant, and provides links to seed sales and customer service.

Johnny's Selected Seeds
www.johnnyseeds.com

This Maine-based, employee-owned company sells organic and heirloom seeds and supplies.

Pests

Aaak! What is that winged thing on my precious baby bean sprout? What is that slime trail? What are these worms doing in my corn stalks? I need some answers, stat!

National Gardening Association: Pest Control Library
www.garden.org/pestlibrary

The National Gardening Association provides "mug shots" of common garden pests and diseases along with information about what to do about them.

Dave's Garden: Integrated Pest Management
davesgarden.com/guides/articles/view/1041

Texas master gardener Tamara Galbraith outlines the principles of integrated pest management, in which we work with the environment to strengthen plants and minimize pests without having to put poison all over everything.

Supplies

Sure, I go to the local hardware store for shovels and such. But I visit these sites for specialty items like raised bed corners and seed tape.

Gardener's Supply Company
www.gardeners.com

Find everything for the gardener from tumbling composters to Botani-wipes. There are gardening advice articles here, too.

Gardens Alive!
www.gardensalive.com

This Indiana company is dedicated to providing organic garden supplies that actually work! Biologically control your pests with their products.

Mailorder Gardening Association
www.mailordergardening.com

Browse the Mailorder Gardening Association database by category to find exactly the right supplier for your gardening needs.

Canning and Preserving Vegetables

Now comes harvest time. My gardening has been successful, and how am I rewarded? With more ripe, delicious vegetables than I can possibly eat before they spoil! No worries. As the saying goes, "We eat what we can, and what we can't, we can." Here's how.

National Center for Home Food Preservation

www.uga.edu/nchfp

Can, freeze, cure, smoke, or ferment: However you can preserve food, this comprehensive website will explain how to do it safely. The National Center for Home Food Processing and Preservation researches and distributes updated information about home food preservation based on both existing studies and ongoing scientific research. Start here for all your food preservation information needs.

Penn State: Home Food Preservation

extension.psu.edu/food-safety/food-preservation

Penn State offers this comprehensive and searchable page as part of its Food Safety website. Search by food name for links to information about preserving particular crops. Also, browse the "Let's Preserve" series, as in "Let's Preserve ... Leafy Greens." Yeah, it's goofy. But the information is airtight.

Freshpreserving.com

www.freshpreserving.com

Jarden Branded Consumables, purveyor of those old Mason jars, offers step-by-step instruction on the traditional art of canning. Find recipes for all sorts of foods that you can "put up." Buy your supplies here, too. Also available in French on its Canadian sister site.

Why Garden?

In his book *What Are People For?* (North Point Press, 1990), philosopher Wendell Berry writes, "How we eat determines, to a considerable extent, how the world is used." Aunt Bert honors this when she makes sure that none of her food is wasted. And, when we grow some of our own produce close to home in compact gardens, we also use the world better.

Take that, economic disaster and climate change!

13

Dedicated Servers:
Cooking and Dining Websites

Marry, 'tis an ill cook that cannot lick his own fingers.
Therefore he that cannot lick his fingers goes not with me.
—Shakespeare, *Romeo and Juliet*, Act 4, Scene 2

It doesn't happen often enough: You visit a restaurant, or a foodie friend. You take a first bite of a new dish. Suddenly, it feels like a capsule of pleasure cracks open to flood its warmth through you, from mouth to loin to toe. This is one of the most delicious things that you have ever eaten! All at once, you realize why people devote so much time and energy to the pursuit of fine food. Eating delicious stuff is one of the great joys of this life.

With the help of the web, it's never been easier to make or buy something good to eat. But of course, sharing recipes is a basic human instinct, as Kathleen Collins points out in her book *Watching What We Eat* (Continuum, 2010). "Cooking instruction has a history as old as that of humans and fire," she writes. The first cookbook was printed in America in 1796. One of the first radio shows was about cooking: Aunt Sammy shared her "Housekeeper's Chat" via wireless starting in 1926. Betty Crocker, a character invented by the Washburn Crosby Company (an outfit that merged with General Mills), gave weekly radio cooking lessons beginning in 1924.

In 1963, Julia Child's show *The French Chef* helped cooking instruction take off on television. In the 1980s, USENET newsgroups such as rec.food.recipes (www.cs.cmu.edu/~mjw/recipes/recipe-index.html) appeared on the text-only internet, shared among the academics who had access to it. The graphical web, which took off in about 1995, was a natural continuum.

Now, we have pictures and videos to show us how to cook, even on our cell phones. We've got abundant advice about restaurant selection. With the web on our side, there is no excuse for a bad meal. So sit back, put your napkin on your lap, and prepare for the best websites for good eats.

Recipes

Betty Crocker's Picture Cookbook (McGraw-Hill, second ed., 1956) was the cooking bible for me and my four little sisters as we grew up in our 1960s Los Angeles suburb. The recipes were hearty but tended toward the heavy and bland. Fortunately, cooking styles have changed since then. Today's recipes are more healthful and much tastier! Here's how to find them.

Epicurious
www.epicurious.com

I don't cook often, but when I do, I turn to this blend of recipes from *Bon Appétit* magazine and the late, great *Gourmet*. Browse recipes by menu, or search particular ingredients to see what you can make out of what you have. Create a free account to store your recipes; you can also print them in several formats. Get a shopping list and then download the whole thing to the free app on your iPhone (www.epicurious.com/services/mobile). Find cooking tips here, too. No matter what I cook from this site, it is always delicious!

Epicurious

Allrecipes.com

allrecipes.com

Says writer Mary Brown, "This is my go-to recipe site. The sheer volume of recipes ensures that I always find what I want, and I get a lot of info from the reviews and ratings." Browse by course or main ingredient. Join the site for free, or purchase a "supporting membership" at about $18 per year to save customized recipes and to hobnob with other cooks online. Choose your dinner menu by slot machine with the $2.99 app for the iPhone, DinnerSpinnerPro (allrecipes.com/features/more/iphone.aspx?linkid=2004&ect=7).

FoodNetwork.com

www.foodnetwork.com

Another cornucopia of recipe delight is the Food Network website. This companion to the cable TV channel offers a general recipe search. Or browse by categories like "Quick & Easy," "Holidays & Parties," or recipes from television chefs such as Paula Deen, Guy Fieri, and Rachel Ray. Watch video clips from the shows. Complete free registration on the site to join contests and store your favorite recipes. Browse the Food Network on your mobile phone browser (foodnetwork.mobi) or download the free iPhone app (itunes.apple.com/app/food-network-nighttime/id332 170282?mt=8).

Food.com

www.food.com

Search among the hundreds of thousands of recipes submitted by devoted foodies. Join for free to upload your own. Registered users can also store, rate, and discuss recipes with others. Food.com is a sister site to the Food Network.

New York Times: Dining & Wine

www.nytimes.com/pages/dining

Browse Gray Lady recipe archives by keyword or from the dropdown "Cooking and Dining Topics" menu based on category ("Quick Appetizers" or "Hanukkah") or food item ("Apples" or "Meatloaf.") Search and view these recipes from your mobile phone web browser (mobile.nytimes.com/recipes).

Lighter Fare

Maybe our problem is too much good food! Not to worry. Even if you suffer from padded library bottom as I do, there are plenty of delicious recipes out there just for us.

Weight Watchers: Food and Recipes

www.weightwatchers.com/food

The recipes are not searchable for non-members. However, you can still view the latest recipes, plus ideas on how to stay slim with tips for shopping and dining out.

Cooking Light

www.cookinglight.com

This online version of *Cooking Light* magazine features a recipe search with light, modern dishes. It also offers cooking instruction articles and ideas for general entertaining. There are also pieces about how to maintain a healthy lifestyle and a place to register and store recipes online. This site links to sister magazines that also serve up tasty, if sometimes heavier recipes: *Southern Living* (www.southernliving.com/food) and *Sunset Magazine* (www.sunset.com/food-wine).

Recipes for Diabetics

Diabetics must control their blood sugar with insulin, by exercising, and by eating foods with a low glycemic load. Here are some of the best sites to help with that.

DLife: For Your Diabetes Life!

www.dlife.com/diabetes/diabetic-recipes

Get your diabetes-friendly recipes here. Browse by category (Course, Main Ingredient, or Dietary restriction) or search for recipes by keyword. Register on the site to store your faves. There is a Food Look-Up tool that offers nutritional information for common foods. Also, find articles here that can help you manage your diet. Diabetic eating is healthy eating!

Diabetes Forecast: Food and Recipes

forecast.diabetes.org/food-recipes

The American Diabetes Association hosts this online magazine to ease diabetic life. Search safe recipes by alphabetic order. Or submit your own recipe to Food Editor Robin Webb. She chooses one submission every week to "Diabetize," that is, change it so it is acceptable in a diabetic diet.

Gluten-Free Recipes

What if you are allergic to the gluten in wheat or other grains? That's called Celiac disease, an autoimmune disorder that attacks the small intestine and can cause malabsorption, which can make you sick and miserable. Fortunately, avoiding gluten will allow the gut to heal.

Carol Fenster's Savory Palate

www.savorypalate.com/recipes.aspx

Colorado's Carol Fenster, PhD, is an authority on cooking well for gluten intolerance. Browse her free recipes here, including those for pizza, cakes, and muffins.

Celiac Sprue Association: Gluten-Free Recipes

www.csaceliacs.org/recipes.php

The Celiac Sprue Association, based in Omaha, Nebraska, offers basic tips for recipe substitutions to make menus gluten-free. Browse its collection of recipes for breads and cakes that are completely devoid of wheat flour. Potato pancakes, anyone?

Other Food Sensitivities

What if gluten is not your problem? What if you have an allergy to, say, sesame seeds? No worries. There are sites that offer recipes that are safe for every sensitivity.

Well-Fed Everyone: Food Allergy Friendly Recipes

wellfedeveryone.wordpress.com/food-allergy-friendly-recipes

New England pastry chef "Margaret" shares a variety of allergy-safe recipes. The recipes are categorized by type (e.g. "Fish" and "Dessert"), and each has a key next to it explaining what allergens it lacks.

Living Without: Gluten-Free, Dairy Free Recipes

www.livingwithout.com/topics/recipes.html

This "magazine for people with allergies and food sensitivities" shows how to make breads, desserts, and entire meals that are safe for those who can't tolerate gluten or milk. The site also hosts plenty of articles about how to cope with all kinds of food allergies.

The Food Allergy & Anaphylaxis Network

www.foodallergy.org

The Food Allergy & Anaphylaxis Network, an advocacy group that raises awareness of food allergies, offers several recipes for free but will open its entire database of yummy dishes to those who become members at $50 per year.

Vegetarian and Vegan Recipes

My vegetarian and vegan friends are as gentle as the animals that they won't eat. But vegetarian and vegan bloggers are as fiercely passionate as they are compassionate. They love to write as much as they love to eat! Here are a mere four of at least a hundred blogs that feature vegan or vegetarian recipes. Look at their blogrolls (that is, the list of blogs that these bloggers follow) to find many more. It's a vegetarian blogapaloosa!

Vegan Explosion

www.veganexplosion.com

"Crystal" from Austin, Texas, creates vegan dishes with a spicy Southwestern flair and then takes beautiful pictures of them. Browse her archive for a list of recipes.

JusttheFood.com

justthefood.blogspot.com

Joni Marie Newman sells real estate in Orange County, California, and writes books about her extraordinary vegan cooking. Click through to her "Quick Links to Recipes." Also, read her

"Secret Ingredients to Avoid" to give a pass to meat products hiding in processed food. Newman also offers handy measurement equivalents on her sidebar. Get ready for "Savory Noodle Kugel Burger."

Our Veggie Kitchen

www.ourveggiekitchen.com

Foodie "Matt," an affordable housing director in Eugene, Oregon, and his wife Kristen dish up their favorite meat substitute recipes.

Andrea's Easy Vegan Cooking

cookeasyvegan.blogspot.com/p/recipes.html

Browse the vegan recipes of Seattle graphic designer "Andrea." Find "Bean and corn fritters," "Chipotle black bean burgers," and "Tofu and kale burritos." She lists recipes for desserts and sides, too.

Food Blogs

What sets food blogs apart from mere recipe databases is not only their kitchen obsession but their exquisite photography. These food blogs make food look so beautiful and delicious that you can't wait to cook it yourself. (You might want to set up some studio lighting in the dining room if you want the same look as the blog photos.)

Here are some of the prettiest blogs.

Smitten Kitchen

smittenkitchen.com

Deb Perelman makes like Julie Powell of the Julie/Julia Project and cooks, cooks, cooks (and then writes and takes stunning photographs) in her tiny NYC apartment. But this blog is not about her. It's about helping you cook food as beautifully and deliciously as she does. Perelman offers advice on how to keep metallic baking powder from ruining your muffins and tips to prevent cookies from spreading. Browse her recipes by season, vegetable, or fruit.

FRIDAY, JUNE 4, 2010
lamb chops with pistachio tapenade

One thing I am realizing about going a long time without eating meat (15 years) followed by a relatively short time eating as a moderately enthusiastic meat eater (5 years and change) is that it doesn't always occur to you to include it in meals. In fact, I have apparently only made four dishes on the site this year that include meat, and two were briskets for big dinner parties. With a fridge bursting (literally; if you can find room for a jar of mayo in there, you'd be my hero) with spinach and scallions, radishes, real baby carrots, sugar snaps, shelling peas and tiny freshly-dug red potatoes rolling off the top, I can hardly imagine why I'd need to roast a chicken. But when I was going through my (very, very, very long) list of Recipes I Want To Try last week, these lamb chops jumped out at me, promising to at least temporarily break me out of my asparagus — hashed! ribboned! tossed with pasta for one! — rut.

Smitten Kitchen

101 Cookbooks

www.101cookbooks.com

Heidi Swanson decided to stop reading and start cooking her way through the over one hundred cookbooks she had collected. Read about her adventures in cooking (mostly with natural and whole foods) and traveling. Browse her recipes by category or ingredient. Most of all, feast your eyes on her gorgeous pictures of food.

Simply Recipes

simplyrecipes.com

There are only a few hundred recipes here, but all have been personally tested by Elise Bauer of Carmichael, California, her mom and dad, or her friends. As a result, you can be sure that every one is a winner. Browse by type or ingredient. Each is accompanied by a lovely photo. Find Simply Recipes on your mobile phone browser (simplyrecipes.com/m).

Cooking Without Shopping

It's all well and good to decide to make a new dish. But sometimes, your choice is limited to the ingredients you have on hand. Visit these sites to find recipes to put those old bananas and that box of elderly pasta to work. Or find an in-house ingredient that can substitute for one called for in the recipe.

Supercook

www.supercook.com

What do you have in the fridge and the pantry? Go ahead and type them in at this site, and Supercook will find recipes that use those ingredients. You can also specify things that you want to leave out of your dish, such as meat or wheat. The search results are tabbed into "Starters," "Entrées," and "Desserts." Register for free to save your recipes on the site.

Recipe Puppy

www.recipepuppy.com

Here is another ingredient-based search engine. Type in the food that you have at hand, separated by commas. Recipe Puppy will fetch suggestions from Food.com and other major sites. It can also search for vegetarian (vegetarianrecipe.us), vegan (veganrecipe. us), or gluten-free recipes (cookglutenfree.net). Recipe Puppy also offers a search by ZIP code of grocery stores that make deliveries and a restaurant coupon search.

The Cook's Thesaurus

www.foodsubs.com

Lori Alden suggests substitutions for thousands of cooking ingredients, including low-calorie and low-fat alternatives for dieters, inexpensive substitutes for gourmets on a budget, and innovative replacements for hard-to-find ethnic ingredients. Very useful!

Learning to Cook

If I'm going to be doing all this fancy work in the kitchen, I'd like to know how to do it right. Here are two instruction sites.

Rouxbe Cooking School

rouxbe.com

Become a better cook with Vancouver's Rouxbe (pronounced "ruby") Cooking School online. There are free video tips for how to properly pan fry foods, for example. (Use a drop of water to gauge the temperature of the pan. The drop should bead and slide around like it was mercury.) Serious students may want to pay $99 per year for access to all the lessons on the site.

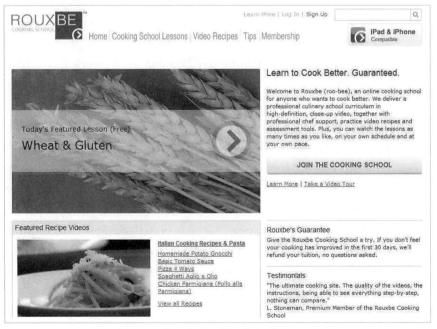

Rouxbe Cooking School

About.com: Culinary Arts

culinaryarts.about.com

Chef Danilo Alfaro covers the fundamentals of the culinary arts, addressing everything from basic food safety to how to whip up a cunning beurre blanc (or butter sauce.) Watch Alfaro's videos demonstrating kitchen procedures, such as how to hone a knife or separate eggs. Read his tutorials for preparing sauces (such as roux), meats, vegetables, and desserts.

Dining Out

All this talk of cooking leaves me exhausted. There's nothing for it but going out to dinner. I'll use these sites to help me find a good restaurant.

Restaurant.com

www.restaurant.com

That old Italian place around the corner? That Thai joint down the street? They may give you a discount! Register for free to check it out on Restaurant.com. Perhaps the fanciest joints in town are not on this list. But you may find that the restaurants you love most will give you a break on your bill.

Yelp

www.yelp.com

Yelp is great for travel, but it works just as well in your home-town. Browse Yelp's user reviews to find a restaurant to suit your mood and budget. Its mobile interface works well on web-enabled cell phones (m.yelp.com). Or download the app for Android, iPhone, or BlackBerry (www.yelp.com/yelpmobile). On my GPS-enabled Android, Yelp gives me a list of nearby restaurants wher-ever I am.

Urbanspoon

www.urbanspoon.com

Shake up your usual dining out routine with Urbanspoon. It helps you find new places to eat with a slot machine interface. Simply shake your iPhone (or push the "shake" button on the Android or BlackBerry), and the free app spins until it finds a restaurant near you. Read restaurant reviews from published sources and from users. Lots of fun! Find your mobile app at www.urbanspoon.com/go_mobile.

Snapfinger

www.snapfinger.com

You know, I can't even bring myself to go out. Who delivers? Snapfinger knows. Enter your city to see which (mostly national chain) restaurants near you deliver or encourage pickup. Order online through the site, a widget on your PC desktop, your mobile phone browser, or via the free iPhone app (itunes.apple.com/us/app/snapfinger-restaurant-ordering/id328071835?mt=8). I wonder if I can get Snapfinger to feed me, too?

Finger Lickin' Good

Shakespeare wrote that we can judge a chef by how often he licks his own fingers, delighting in his own creation. I hope that these foodie websites keep us licking our fingers for years to come! But just don't get crumbs on the keyboard.

14

Remote Access:
Travel on the Web

I fear you have sold your own lands to see other men's;
then to have seen much and to have nothing is to have
rich eyes and poor hands.

—Shakespeare, *As You Like It*, Act 4, Scene 1

To gain "rich eyes," as Shakespeare put it, with travel is one of the
great joys of life. The web has made it much easier to arrange our
trips, to save money, to find our way, and generally make our travel
experience much smoother. These tools let us have fun without
ending up with "poor hands!"

Online Travel Agents

A good place to start planning a simple trip is with one on the four
giant internet travel sites: Travelocity, Expedia, Orbitz, and
Priceline. These "portals" pull everything together: flight reservations, travel guides, and anything else the traveler might need.
Choose one as your home, or search among several to find the best
prices and fit for your needs.

181

For a complicated international excursion, it still may be best to work with a flesh-and-blood professional travel agent. Still, these sites can give you an overview about cost and activities.

Travelocity

www.travelocity.com

Travelocity is owned and powered by the SABRE Group, which operates the major travel agent reservation database. Through Travelocity, you can book and monitor flight, car, and hotel reservations for domestic or international trips. Purchase railway tickets, tour packages, and cruises here, too. Sign up to get trip ideas and for notifications when fares drop. Travelocity will also work for you to help smooth travel snafus. Find them on your web-enabled cell phone at mobile.travelocity.com.

Expedia

www.expedia.com

Expedia was born as Microsoft's attempt to knock Travelocity out of the sky. Now it is a stand-alone, full-service travel company that offers hotel, car, cruise, and airline reservations. Expedia also owns Hotels.com, Hotwire.com, TripAdvisor, and SeatGuru.

Orbitz

www.orbitz.com

Book your trip through Orbitz, a Chicago-based, full-service, online travel agency. Like Travelocity and Expedia, Orbitz features flight, car, hotel, cruise, and Amtrak ticketing services. In addition, tickets for shows, attractions, and even ski lifts can be bought here. Orbitz also owns CheapTickets and GORP, a guide for outdoor adventures in the U.S.

Priceline

www.priceline.com

Connecticut's Priceline is famous for its spokesman, William Shatner, who karate chops travel rates for savvy consumers. The site's "Name Your Own Price" feature is for the flexible traveler. Here, you place a "bid" stating the price that you wish to pay for a ticket, a car rental, or hotel room. If your bid is accepted, you are bound to buy the ticket, even if, for example, the flight travels at an inconvenient time or includes a stopover. Those who want more control can choose specific flights and hotels at less amazing although still discounted rates. Book attraction tickets and even ground transportation here, too. Priceline operates in 90 countries and 32 languages. Download the free hotel reservation app to your iPhone to save money on the go (itunes.apple.com/app/priceline-hotel-negotiator/id336381998?mt=8).

Price Comparisons

Get a feel for current ticket prices by running your plans through these fare-comparison search engines.

KAYAK

www.kayak.com

Before you make any hasty reservation decisions, be sure to run your travel search through KAYAK. The site combs more than 500 travel sites for the best rates. Set up fare alerts to let you know if ticket prices take a tumble. Search KAYAK on your iPhone, Android smart phone, or BlackBerry with apps (www.kayak.com/iphone).

Bing Travel

www.bing.com/travel

Compare airline ticket prices in a graph format. Like a stock chart, the "Price Predictor" graph shows the tendency of ticket prices and advises the best time to buy.

Travelzoo

www.travelzoo.com

This is a great place to find deals on international vacations. Historian Mike Monroney of Aspen, Colorado, advises, "Travelzoo is a great source for ideas: Looking over what they offer, I often come up with destinations I hadn't thought about." He discovered the tour company Friendly Planet (www.friendly planet.com) through Travelzoo's "Top 20" email. "I used them to go to China, Thailand, and Egypt," he says. Travelzoo also offers fare-comparison searches for flights, hotels, cruises, and car rentals. Scan the News Flash and Last Minute feeds to catch bargains as they appear.

Travel Guides

Visiting a new place is exciting but can also be scary. On these sites, fellow travelers and professionals give you a preview of what to expect on your trip.

TripAdvisor

www.tripadvisor.com

When I plan a vacation, my first stop is TripAdvisor. I love their overviews of vacation spots and thoughtful reviews of specific hotels and attractions written by users. For example, when my family stayed in Flagstaff, Arizona, we knew to bring earplugs because reviewers mentioned that the train runs right through town night and day. TripAdvisor links to booking services, too, with searches for hotels, flights, and even vacation condo rentals. The site adapts easily to your mobile phone web browser. Or download the TripAdvisor app for Android, Palm Pre, or iPhone (www.trip advisor.com/InfoCenter-a_ctr.mobile).

TripAdvisor

Fodor's Travel

www.fodors.com

Travel is so much fun when you understand what you are looking at! Get the background information that you need from Fodor's, which has published terrific travel guides since 1936. The website offers travel and cultural tips for destinations across the world along with basic travel phrases in several languages. (Most important: "Puis-je me connecter à l'internet?" translates to "Can I connect to the internet?") Fodors.com adapts to your web-enabled cell phone automatically.

DK Travel

traveldk.com

Dorling Kindersley publishes the beloved picture-packed travel guides. Buy one here or register with the site to make your own, fashioned specifically for your trip. Share the result online or print it out to take it with you. For about $8, download a "Top 10" guide for any one of a variety of popular destinations to your iPhone.

Frommer's Travel Guides

www.frommers.com

Frommer's guides have helped travelers since Arthur Frommer first published *Europe on $5 a Day* in 1957. Find all kinds of useful information on the site including trip ideas, news about travel deals, and even health insurance for travelers. Download the free Frommer's Travel Tools app to your iPhone (itunes.apple.com/us /app/id366011058?mt=8). You'll find a currency converter, a tip calculator, and even a way to make your phone act like a flashlight.

Rick Steves' Europe Through the Back Door

www.ricksteves.com

Don't visit Europe without Rick Steves. Plan your trip and get travel tips from Steves and his loyal fans. Book a tour and purchase rail passes. Buy suitcases and other travel gear. Listen to Steves' audio tours of Europe on the site (www.ricksteves.com/radio/tgr/ tgr_menu.htm) or download them into iTunes.

Web Tips for a Smoother Flight

"Beware the myth of easy travel," a friend once cautioned. His warning seems increasingly apt as security measures put in place after 9/11 and airline cutbacks have made traveling by air an oddly hostile experience, more of an ordeal than an adventure.

Just as it helps us to find the cheapest air fares, the internet can also deliver the data we need to reach our destination without disaster. Many travel websites also work on web-enabled mobile phones or can deliver text messages. That's a great advantage for the traveler on the go who can't always get to a computer to connect to the internet.

To avoid becoming a victim of the chaos of unregulated airlines and outdated air traffic control equipment, it helps to be informed about the current state of affairs: on the ground, in the air, and on the plane.

FlightStats

www.flightstats.com

This comprehensive website dishes up all sorts of handy real-time flight information and delivers it in a variety of ways: on the site, through an RSS feed, and via cell phone—all for free. Search between destinations to see what flights are offered and if they have any available seats. No ticket price data here, but you will get historical on-time flight ratings.

FlightStats offers general airport delay information, airport maps with weather radar overlays, and real-time Google traffic information. Its flight tracker matches flights to gates and even lets you know when a plane has pushed away from its gate but has not

FlightStats

yet taken off. If you forget to check FlightStats on your home computer, pick it up on your web-enabled cell phone at the terminal (mobile.flightstats.com).

SeatGuru
www.seatguru.com

Now you know about the airport, but what about the plane? SeatGuru will reveal the pros and cons of your assigned seat, even telling you if it offers a plug for your laptop. To research on the run, type mobile.seatguru.com into your web-enabled phone browser or PDA.

Transportation Security Administration: For Travelers
www.tsa.gov/travelers

Of course, the state of your seat won't matter if you can't get through airport security. Visit this site for tips to speed you through. Find out how much shampoo you can bring aboard, understand why you can't bring your snow globe in your carry-on, and learn procedures for bringing along prescription medicines.

Now you are totally prepared. You know your airport and airline, and you have printed out your ticket. Unfortunately, that ticket does not guarantee the flight.

To save money, airlines have been canceling flights like crazy, and sometimes they don't notify passengers ahead of time. What steps can you take to make sure that you don't get a nasty surprise at the airport?

Travel writer Chris Elliott (www.elliott.org) says that the best way to avoid this plight is to book through a reliable travel agent. These professionals are savvy to the state of specific airlines and know which ones are cutting back. If you are a "do-it-yourselfer," Elliot suggests enrolling in your airline's email alert system—but just make sure that the messages don't go into the spam filter. Also, check historical flight information on FlightStats (mentioned earlier) to see whether this particular flight is often canceled or if the airport often experiences delays.

Finally, check your reservations at least two weeks in advance, before you have to pay the inflated "walk-up" fare for a replacement. If you read the news and sense that your flight may be canceled, proactively call the airline; check Airline Contact Information (airlinecontact.info).

Seems like a lot of work for something that you assumed was settled once you handed over your credit card. Still, in this tight transportation environment, it is better to be cautious than to spend half of your vacation at the airport Cinnabon instead of in Hawaii.

Free Wi-Fi

No matter where I travel, I feel cut off if I can't connect to the internet. Most hotels understand this and offer free web access. But as librarian and road warrior mom Cheryl Tarsala warned in a personal email after she took a cross-country car trip recently, "You need to read info about hotels carefully. Really expensive ones charge extra for Wi-Fi—the Hyatt doesn't even tell you this upfront."

So, say your hotel Wi-Fi is pricey or nonexistent. What do you do? "Travelers' hint," writes Cheryl. "Food places with bakery goods have an incentive to lure you in with free Wi-Fi." Just take your computer out for a pastry and a cup of joe (or a cuppa in the U.K.). Starbucks, anyone?

JiWire Global

v4.jiwire.com/search-hotspot-locations.htm

Use the interactive world map at this site to zoom in on locations, or type a known city or ZIP code in the search box to find a mix of pay and free access points across the globe. Use the advanced search feature to filter for free sites only. iPhone and wireless iPod touch users can download an application (www.jiwire.com/iphone) that will sense either paid wireless internet access points or just those that offer free access. Indeed, Tarsala was right: Many bakeries appear on JiWire's maps.

Wi-Fi-FreeSpot

wififreespot.com

Here is another directory of free internet access points. U.S. travelers can browse state-by-state listings or view a directory of restaurant and hotel chains that make it policy to keep customers connected to the web for free. Another page lists free access in Europe (wififreespot.com/europe.html).

Perkins Restaurant & Bakery

www.perkinsrestaurants.com/locations

Use this site to find Perkins Restaurants across the U.S. and Canada. Says Tarsala, "Perkins has free Wi-Fi, and they are open 24 hours in some locations, especially weekends."

Panera Bread: Free Wi-Fi Hotspots

www.panerabread.com/cafes/wifi.php

This growing franchise already has more than 1,250 shops offering bread and free internet access across the U.S. Tarsala found Panera a tasty and welcome respite on the road. "Between Perkins and Panera, we have crossed the country."

Cell Phones Abroad

You must have a cell phone to keep in touch on the road. But there's a problem. Chances are your American cell phone will not work when you travel abroad. And even if it does, using it there is like calling from here—expensive. No matter what, the international traveler will need to spend some money to have cell phone access abroad.

Rick Steves' Europe: Mobile Phones and Smart Phones in Europe

www.ricksteves.com/plan/tips/mobilephones.htm

Travel expert Rick Steves offers a lucid explanation of the complicated business of using a cell phone in Europe. Europe uses a transmission standard called GSM (Global System for Mobile Communications). In the U.S., most companies operate on a network called CDMA (code division multiple access), which doesn't work abroad. The exceptions are T-Mobile and AT&T, which do use GSM. GSM phones hold a little chip behind the battery. This chip, called a SIM (subscriber identity module) card, contains the phone's memory, including its number and location. An American-based GSM phone on the AT&T network, for example, could work in Europe. But because the SIM card is U.S.-based, it would rack up international calling rates anywhere but home. Not only that, every time you cross a border in Europe, you get smacked with "roaming" charges. To avoid these, you must literally buy a new SIM card for every country that you visit.

What to do? Here are some suggestions.

Rick Steves' Europe: Mobile Phones and Smart Phones in Europe

Slow Travel: Cell Phones in Europe
www.slowtrav.com/europe/cell_phones.htm

Pauline Kenny outlines the choices available for U.S. citizens who want to use a cell phone, aka *mobile phone* or *handy*, in Europe. She details the steps needed to swap out SIMs. She also recommends companies that rent cell phones to travelers and explains how to actually dial a phone number in distant lands—including the international codes.

Independent Traveler: International Cell Phone Guide
www.independenttraveler.com/resources/article.cfm?AID=552& category=3

Caroline Costello explains the options available to Americans who feel naked without a cell phone on their travels. She cautions, "Expensive cell phones can easily get lost or stolen in another country, and an American chatting on a pricey mobile phone can be a target for thieves." Reason enough to rent or buy a cheap model!

Finally, if you want to talk for a long time to loved ones at home, you can always bypass the cell phone altogether. Instead, use Google Chat (www.google.com/talk) or Skype (www.skype. com) on a computer connected to the internet.

Other Useful Travel Sites

The web hosts an array of indispensable tools for the traveler. Here's a selection.

Google Maps
maps.google.com

How far is it? How long will it take? I need directions. What's the traffic like? What will the street scene look like when I arrive? What did we do before Google Maps? This completely satisfying service is available as an app on iPhone, Android, and BlackBerry, or pull down the service on your mobile browser (www.google.com/mobile/maps).

Need directions but your phone is not so smart? No problem. Just dial 1-800-GOOG-411 (1-800-466-4411). A voice will ask you where you are and what you are looking for. "Pizza," you respond. Google will read a list of pizzerias in your area. Choose the one you want, and Google will put a call through to them free of charge. You can say "text message" to have business contact information sent to your cell phone via SMS. Is that cool or what? Type that phone number into your lists of contacts right now!

Luggage Free

luggagefree.com

Airline baggage fees: Hate 'em! I don't care to drag big bags through the airport, either. And if the airline loses my luggage, it has lost me as a customer for keeps. One possible solution: For as little as a dollar a pound, I can have luggage shipped to my destination. No need to take it with me on the plane! Luggage Free picks up and delivers bags where I want, when I want, including to cruise ships and hotels. I'll never lug those golf clubs through the airport ever again!

RoadsideAmerica.com

www.roadsideamerica.com

As you drive across the U.S. with your family, use Roadside America.com to make sure that you see all of the weird stuff that folks set up across our nation. In Fanning, Missouri, be amazed at the World's Largest Rocking Chair. Thrill to the giant Van Gogh painting in Goodland, Kansas. Cower at the foot of the World's Largest Garden Gnome in Ames, Iowa. Need to keep track of the strangeness on the go? Download the RoadsideAmerica.com iPhone app for one of six U.S. regions for about $3. You get the whole nation in one download for $9 (www.roadsideamerica.com/mobile).

Atlas Obscura

atlasobscura.com

Find curiosities and esoteric spots on your travels around the world. Search by destination.

Weather Underground

www.wunderground.com

The Weather Underground lets you know what it will be like where you are going and will even give you driving directions for getting there. Find webcams here for real-time weather views. Weather Underground gets its data from more than 13,000 private weather stations from around the world. Point your web-enabled cell phone to its mobile site (m.wund.com) or with the free WunderMap for the iPhone (itunes.apple.com/us/app/wunder map/id364884105?mt=8).

Travel.State.Gov

travel.state.gov

The U.S. Department of State presents a heaping helping of helpful information for international travelers on its handsome site, including instructions for applying for or renewing a passport. It can also warn you if your destination target has turned dangerous.

Travel Apps

Apps are perfect for travel. Here are some that can make travel easier.

TripCase App

www.tripcase.com

This free app, for Windows Mobile, BlackBerry, or iPhone, urges us to "get a handle on our travel." Enter your itinerary into this tiny, powerful program; it will let you know the status of your flight and suggest others if yours is canceled. It will even pull in security wait times. The app also lets you share travel photos and notes with friends.

TripIt App

www.tripit.com

This app's strength lies in its social connections. Share your travel plans with your colleagues and friends; you can also track them on a map. Its free app comes in three free flavors: iPhone, Android, and BlackBerry (www.tripit.com/uhp/mobile). You can also find the site with your mobile web browser (m.tripit.com /home).

Yelp App

www.yelp.com/yelpmobile or m.yelp.com

Yelp offers reviews of mainly U.S. restaurants and services written by users. Search for restaurants and spas by keyword, category, or neighborhood. The Yelp app for the smart phones, BlackBerry, iPhone, Palm Pre, and Android works very well (www.yelp.com/yelpmobile). Or just pull it in on your mobile phone browser (m.yelp.com).

Urbanspoon App

www.urbanspoon.com/blackberry or
itunes.apple.com/app/urbanspoon/id284708449?mt=8 or
www.urbanspoon.com/android

UrbanSpoon, an alternative to Yelp, comes with the added fun of a slot machine interface. Simply shake your iPhone (or push the "shake" button on the Android or BlackBerry), and the free app spins until it finds a good restaurant near you. Reviews come from published sources and from users. It works in London and Sydney, too.

Bon Voyage!

Now that you have perfectly planned your trip with the help of the web and smart phone apps, I can bid you bon voyage. "Look you lisp and wear strange suits," as Shakespeare advised, "or I will scarce think you have swam in a gondola."

15

Fur E-Friends:
Internet Information for Pets

When he was 7 years old, my son Peter didn't just want a dog, he craved one. Pining for a canine dominated his world. It came to rule ours too, as, with the lawyerly skill of the young, he argued all angles of the advantages of dog ownership to us, his parents, assailing us day and night with logic that could stand in the Supreme Court. But we already had two cats, a middle-aged tom and an ancient female who had come to live with me back in my dating days.

We used the "cranky old cat" excuse to forestall dog adoption and, actually, our cat Helen *was* developing a few health problems, although she didn't seem very ill. I was reluctant to take her to the vet, imagining that the doctor would order procedures that were expensive but ultimately ineffective. At the time, I just wanted her to be more "regular," if you know what I mean. So I turned to the web for some pet health advice.

Pet Information and Supplies

The web overflows with pet health information and advice, both authoritative and merely anecdotal. I typed *feline constipation* into

Google and brought up information about a condition called "megacolon." I found a reliable-looking site that recommended feeding the cat canned pumpkin, which is full of fiber and which animals apparently love (www.peteducation.com/article.cfm?c=1+ 2122&aid=3471). I just happened to have a can left over from the previous Thanksgiving. Sure enough, Helen slurped it right up, and it seemed to solve her problem. (Most veterinary sites, by the way, strongly advise taking a constipated cat to the vet. The condition can be very dangerous.)

Of the hearty variety of sites that offer quality information about pet care, most feature sections focused on geriatric animals—perfect for Helen!

MedlinePlus: Pet Health

www.nlm.nih.gov/medlineplus/pethealth.html

MedlinePlus is the jumping off place for human and animal health information. Right off the bat, the site lists seven signs that it's time to take the pet to the vet, including loss of appetite, drinking lots of water, and "strange lumps." Pet Health links to authoritative articles about nutrition, prevention and screening, and specific pet diseases.

American Veterinary Medical Association: Care for Animals

www.avma.org/careforanimals

The American Veterinary Medical Association (AVMA) offers information about pet health, covering cats, dogs, horses, and diseases. There are guides to animal safety and tips on traveling with pets. AVMA also features articles about how to choose a pet and how to deal with the death of an animal friend.

PetEducation.com

www.peteducation.com

This site began as a way for two Wisconsin vets, Drs. Race Foster and Marty Smith, to keep their patients informed and also to sell pet supplies. It has grown into a comprehensive guide to issues concerning all manner of pets: dogs and cats, yes, but also reptiles, birds, fish, ferrets, and "small pets" (e.g., hamsters). Search the site or browse individual articles such as "Barbering in Mice." The medical articles include bibliographies.

American Animal Hospital Association: HealthyPet.com
www.healthypet.com

The American Animal Hospital Association, an organization of more than 29,000 veterinary care providers, brings you this searchable collection of frequently asked questions ("What's wrong with my hedgehog?") and an extensive Pet Care Library. Library topics including common health problems, illness and disease, and pet care tips.

American Society for the Prevention of Cruelty to Animals
www.aspca.org

The American Society for the Prevention of Cruelty to Animals (ASPCA) is the oldest humane organization established in the Western Hemisphere. Visit the site of this venerable institution for information about a variety of pet issues, especially accidental poisoning. The ASPCA Animal Poison Control Center has information available through the site as well as providing around-the-clock veterinary diagnostic and treatment recommendations to those helping animals exposed to potentially hazardous substances. An example: Did you know that eating grapes could cause renal failure in dogs?

The Humane Society of the United States: Pets
www.humanesociety.org/animals/pets

The Humane Society offers some great articles about pet care issues (such as what to do about a dog that digs in the yard) as well as pet adoption advice. Receive its enewsletter or get alerts via text message.

ASPCA

PetMD iPhone App Center

www.petmd.com/iPhone

Download the free PetMD iPhone apps to locate dog services in your area, assess dog symptoms, and administer first aid to a dog or cat.

1800PetMeds

www.1800petmeds.com

This Florida-based site bills itself as "America's Largest Pet Pharmacy." It is easy to use. First, search for your vet in its database. Next, the site contacts the doctor and arranges the prescription. Then the medicine is delivered via snail mail. (Note that because veterinarians often earn income from filling prescriptions at the clinic, they may be reluctant to give them out for use online.)

PetFoodDirect.com

www.petfooddirect.com

Save time and money by buying supplies for all your pets online. Get dog or cat food delivered in bulk on an automatic schedule. Find supplies for horses, fish, and even pet lizards. Afraid to use your credit card online? You can actually call this Pennsylvania-based company at 1-877-PET-FOOD to talk to a person.

Cats

They say dogs have owners; cats have staff. Here are some sites helpful to feline personal assistants.

About.com: Cats

cats.about.com

Franny Syufy writes about all aspects of cat care, including training, "cat proofing" the home, and advice about removing cat urine odor.

Cat Fanciers' Association, Inc.

www.cfainc.org/caring.html

The Cat Fanciers' Association, Inc., founded in 1906, not only sponsors cat shows but is dedicated to working for the good of all cats by sponsoring feline health research and providing disaster relief over the years. Visit its site for breed descriptions and solid links to articles about cat illnesses and treatments.

American Association of Feline Practitioners: Cat Health Topics

www.catvets.com/healthtopics

The American Association of Feline Practitioners offers articles on cat medical conditions and nursing advice as well as general cat wellness information.

Dogster

Dogs

Here are choice resources about man's best friend.

Dogster

www.dogster.com

Visit Dogster to learn about the health and care of your pooch, different breeds, and where to adopt a dog. This is a great site for all things canine.

About.com: Dogs

dogs.about.com

Krista Mifflin, a trainer and caretaker of dogs with special needs, brings us this site chockablock with dog resources. Find general information about dogs, dog breeds, and an index of dog rescue organizations.

Adopting a Pet

Reading about cute pups did make me want to adopt a dog. But how could I find one?

Petfinder

www.petfinder.com

Looking for a dog, cat, bird, reptile, horse, or just something small and furry? Use this site to search through more than 127,000 adoptable pets. Also, browse through Petfinder's online resource library to learn more about caring for pets.

Adopt-A-Pet.com

www.adoptapet.com

Search local shelters for dogs and cats based on breed, gender, age, or just general "type" (e.g. "Eddie and Frasier's Friends" or "Taco Bell Dog's Little Amigos").

Animal Planet: Dog Breed Selector

animal.discovery.com/breedselector/dogselectorindex.do

Animal Planet, from the Discovery channel, offers this multi-choice questionnaire to help users decide which dog breeds might suit them best. My choices (which leaned toward medium-sized, mellow, family friendly characteristics) yielded 55 possible breed matches. Whippet, anyone? Animal Planet also hosts a Cat Breed Selector (animal.discovery.com/breedselector/catselectorindex.do).

The Poop: Rescue Group Database

www.thepoop.com/search_main.asp

Choose your state and the breed of dog that you fancy. The Poop will connect you to the appropriate rescue group near you.

Training Your Pet

Dogs, like children, rely on us to teach them how to behave. Fortunately, training animals has never been easier, especially with resources like these available on the web.

Karen Pryor Clickertraining.com

www.clickertraining.com

Karen Pryor wrote the excellent training book *Don't Shoot the Dog: The New Art of Teaching and Training* (Ringpress, 3rd ed., 2002) that explains the tenets of operant conditioning. This is the basis of "clicker training," which differs in a number of ways from standard or traditional dog training. "First, although we often use food as a primary reinforcer, we use no deprivation," writes Pryor. "Second, we use no punishment within the shaping. Third, the sessions are very brief." Pryor offers clicker training supplies and instruction books for sale on her site as well as basic clicking lessons for free.

Cesar's Way

www.cesarsway.com

"Dog Whisperer" Cesar Millan's full video lessons are available online starting at $13 per month. Download Millan's free iPhone app, "Cesar Says" (itunes.apple.com/us/app/id332616900?mt=8) to hear his signature phrases and to make your phone say, "Tsst" when you shake it.

Association of Pet Dog Trainers: Information for Pet Owners

www.apdt.com/petowners

The Association of Pet Dog Trainers offers training tips for owners. Search for a local trainer here. Also, read helpful articles about socializing dogs with other dogs, in dog parks, for example.

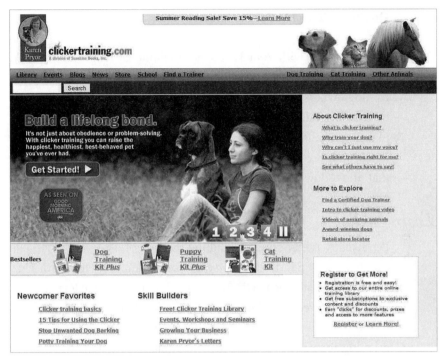

Karen Pryor Clickertraining.com

Traveling With Pets

Just because you have adopted a pet doesn't mean that you'll never leave the house again. When you travel, you might even want to take your pet with you. Here are some sites that can help.

Petswelcome.com

www.petswelcome.com

Which hotel chains, amusement parks, and ski resorts in the U.S., Canada, Great Britain, and France welcome both you and your pets? Explore the "pet-friendly universe" of lodgings in the U.S. and abroad, along with kennel listings and tips for traveling with animals.

DogFriendly.com

www.dogfriendly.com

"Go Places with Your Dog!" is the motto of DogFriendly.com, Inc., a leading provider of nationwide city guides and travel guides for dog owners. "We do not believe that a well-behaved dog should be discriminated against and therefore we focus on listing only places that allow dogs of all sizes and breeds." Find all kinds of cities, lodgings, restaurants, and beaches in the U.S. and Canada that allow dogs.

Losing a Pet

I'm usually pretty good at handling the loss of a pet, but when our cat Helen took a turn for a worse and passed on, it hit me hard. That afternoon, I had to leave the reference desk to wash the tears off my face. In the evening, I just sat on the living room couch and cried.

I felt relieved to find extensive resources on the web about grieving for pets. I suppose it makes sense. Few dogs or cats live more than 20 years. That means that serial pet owners will endure several losses as the decades pass. Here are some sites addressing grief over a pet's death.

AVMA: Pet Euthanasia

www.avma.org/animal_health/brochures/euthanasia/pet/
pet_euth_brochure.asp

The AVMA knows the way to comfort owners about euthanasia, counseling, "Try to recall and treasure the good times you spent with your pet." The vets give good advice about how to know when to put a suffering pet out of its misery.

ASPCA: End-of-Life Care FAQ

www.aspca.org/pet-care/pet-loss/end-of-life-care-faq.html

The ASPCA offers up-to-date information about assessing a pet to determine if it is in pain or dying. They even address the developing trend for pet hospice. "Pet parents" are invited to call the

ASPCA Pet Loss Hotline at 877-474-3310 for help in coping with the death of a pet.

Cornell University: Pet Loss Support Hotline
www.vet.cornell.edu/org/petloss/Resources

Want to talk to a vet student about the loss of your pet? Call the Pet Loss Support Hotline at the Cornell University College of Veterinary Medicine (www.vet.cornell.edu; 607-253-3932), staffed from 6:00 to 9:00 PM Tuesdays through Thursdays. Other veterinary schools that offer pet loss hotlines include the College of Veterinary Medicine at Washington State University (www.vetmed.wsu.edu/PLHl), University of Florida Veterinary Hospitals (www.vetmed.ufl.edu/patientcare/petlosssupport), and University of Illinois College of Veterinary Medicine (vetmed. illinois.edu/CARE).

Missing Pet Network: Finding a Lost Pet—Where to Start
www.missingpet.net/advice

What if your pet is not dead but only missing? The Missing Pet Network, a volunteer group sponsored by the U.S. Department of Agriculture's Animal Care Office, outlines the most effective actions for recovering a lost animal.

PetRescue.com: How to Find a Lost Cat or Dog
www.petrescue.com/petlibrary/pet-rescue/how-to-find-a-lost-cat-or-dog

Florida's PetRescue.com recommends walking the neighborhood and thoroughly searching your property to find your lost pet. They also suggest placing a pile of dirty gym clothes outside your house. Animals, it turns out, find their way home through smell as well as sight.

Peter and the Dog

So what about my son Peter and the dog? Months of his nagging about bringing home a doggie to love ended abruptly when my husband asked Peter just before his eighth birthday, "Would you rather have a puppy or satellite TV?"

Pete hesitated for only a fraction of a second. "Satellite TV," he answered definitively.

That was that. We never heard another word about a dog. Oh well. We make do by watching Animal Planet on the flat screen. Fetch me the remote, would you?

Part Five

Staying Healthy and Happy

The Roman poet Juvenal (c. 55 A.D.) wrote, "Mens sana in corpore sano," meaning that our highest hope in this life should be to have a sound mind in a healthy body. What was true then applies today, and it's a lot easier because we have so many reliable websites to help us improve our health and well-being.

16

Anti-Virus:
Online Medical and Health Information

Our remedies oft in ourselves do lie,
Which we ascribe to heaven.

—Shakespeare,
All's Well That Ends Well, Act 1, Scene 1

The web has completely changed the way we manage our health. Think about it: Before 1995, if we wanted to learn about a disease or condition, we would have to go to a library to read a book. Nothing wrong with that, usually. Still, advances in medicine happen so quickly that half of what a doctor learns is out of date five years after he or she leaves medical school. If it takes several years to publish a medical book and even one or two years to get a medical article to print in a leading journal, how can the information in it be current—or even correct?

Today all of us have instant free access to the latest medical news and research online. We can play detective with our symptoms to see if we need to consult a physician. After a diagnosis, we can read about treatments and possible outcomes. We can research medications so we can, as the commercials say, "Ask

211

your doctor." And if we need the absolute latest in experimental treatments to save our lives, we can use the web to find and enroll in a clinical trial.

The web empowers us to take charge of our health. As Judy Consales, director of the Biomedical Library at UCLA, has pointed out, "When patients are informed about their diseases and treatments, their health care progresses better."

Checking Your Symptoms

You've come down with something, that's for sure. Your throat hurts or you feel nauseous. Maybe you have a cough or a headache that you can't shake. Or your knee clicks. Or your shoulder hurts.

Is it serious enough to go to the doctor? Or will a couple of ibuprofen ease your discomfort until it clears up on its own? Perhaps the first place to start is with a symptom checker.

WebMD: Symptom Checker

symptoms.webmd.com

When my teen's throat started hurting badly, I was convinced that he had a virus. "Squirt it with Chloraseptic," I advised. He wants to be a doctor, so he took his symptoms to the WebMD Symptom Checker to diagnose himself. "Take me to the clinic," he demanded. Sure enough, he had raging strep throat, a bacterial infection which easily succumbed to antibiotics. "Told you," he croaked.

Of course, health information on the web is never a substitute for professional medical advice. Still, in this case, the symptom checker prompted me to get proper and timely treatment for my boy.

General Health Information

Once we figured out what was wrong with him, I wanted to learn about the usual course of this disease and its treatment. So I turned to trustworthy websites to find out more.

MedlinePlus

MedlinePlus

medlineplus.gov

Talk about your tax dollars at work! The National Library of Medicine has brought all its research findings and information together in one spot. Get general overviews and news about health problems along with links to condition-specific official organizations such as the American Heart Association (www.heart.org). Find drug information here and videos of actual surgeries. This is a wonderful starting place for any medical question. We use it at the library reference desk all the time.

Mayo Clinic

www.mayoclinic.com

Oh, Mayo Clinic of Minnesota, how we trust you to give us reliable, comprehensive information about all sorts of ailments, as well as information on drugs, supplements, tests, and procedures. There are healthy lifestyle tools here, too, along with another symptom checker.

FamilyDoctor.org

familydoctor.org

Count on the American Academy of Family Physicians (www.aafp.org) to bring us dependable consumer health information on the wide variety of conditions and ailments that a family doctor might encounter. Visit the OTC Guide to understand the active ingredients in the medications that you can buy over the counter. Browse the Smart Patient Guide for advice about talking to doctors and finding affordable health care. Watch short videos about health problems and solutions.

The Merck Manuals Online Medical Library:
Home Edition for Patients & Caregivers

www.merck.com/mmhe

When doctors need to know about illness, they turn to *The Merck Manual of Diagnosis and Therapy*. But laypeople, the patients and their caregivers, also need clear current information about what ails us and what to do about it. The Home Edition, free and searchable, is for us! In addition to facts about disease, it also gives information about common health tests: what they are for and what the results mean. It will even pronounce medical words out loud so that we can, too, without sounding stupid. Say it with me now: "oligodendroglioma."

Health Organizations for Specific Conditions and Diseases

Craig Haynes, head of the Medical Center Library at the University of California, San Diego, states, "There are scores of nationally recognized, peer-reviewed, professional healthcare associations and government agencies with a clear and defining presence on the web."

These associations and agencies offer tremendous amounts of information about specific diseases and conditions. If you suffer

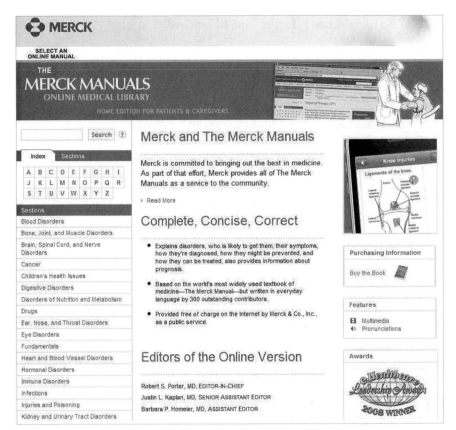

The Merck Manuals Online Medical Library

from a common condition, there is undoubtedly a large advocacy group on the web just for you.

Cardiovascular and Lung Disease

We're all going to die, and most likely it will be from heart disease, according to the Centers for Disease Control and Prevention (www.cdc.gov/nchs/fastats/deaths.htm). Or, although we don't hear about this very much, we could succumb to respiratory problems, which are the fourth leading cause of death in this country. Stroke comes in at number three. Learn to prevent or manage these potentially fatal conditions on the following sites.

National Heart, Lung, and Blood Institute
www.nhlbi.nih.gov

This branch of the National Heart, Lung, and Blood Institute offers patient information about heart disease, blood and blood vessel problems, and lung disorders. Get the skinny on narrowed arteries here along with heart-healthy recipes.

American Heart Association
www.heart.org

Learn about the warning signs of heart attack and stroke and what to do about them. There is also plenty of advice about how to maintain a heart-healthy diet and lifestyle.

COPD Foundation
www.copdfoundation.org

It's emphysema. It's chronic obstructive bronchitis. Wait! Both are right. It's chronic obstructive pulmonary disease (COPD), a progressive condition for which there are treatments but no cure. Learn how to cope with COPD here.

American Lung Association
www.lungusa.org

The American Lung Association (ALA) covers four major lung conditions: asthma, influenza, COPD, and lung cancer. Research your pulmonary problem using the Lung Disease Finder (www.lungusa.org/lung-disease/finder.html). Or call a lung expert at the ALA for advice: 1-800-LUNGUSA. There are registered nurses and registered respiratory therapists who can help you with lung treatment questions.

Cancer

Cancer is the number two killer in the U.S., second only to heart disease. Why is it so prevalent? Well, as treatments for heart problems and other diseases improve, there is little else to make us ill.

But when our own cells mutate and then multiply out of control, invading other tissues and spreading throughout the body, we've got a problem that comes from within: cancer. And because these are our own cells on a rampage, our immune system doesn't recognize them as foreign and lets them grow.

It's a scary thought. Still, scientists work constantly to find new approaches to cure or control this dreadful condition. Here are some sites with cancer-fighting information.

National Cancer Institute

www.cancer.gov

If you or someone you love has been diagnosed with cancer, visit this site first. The National Cancer Institute gives general information for more than 100 types of cancer, as well as links to clinical trials and dictionaries of cancer and drug terms.

American Cancer Society

www.cancer.org

Deciding which treatment is best for your cancer is often confusing. By registering with the American Cancer Society, you get access to its Treatment Decision Tools, which can help determine the most effective course of action. There is also guidance for finding the best doctors and cancer centers, along with nutrition advice for cancer sufferers.

Cancer.Net

www.cancer.net

Will your cancer kill you? Maybe not, if you get the latest treatments. And who knows more about those than the American Society of Clinical Oncology? Get tips on how to track down a cutting-edge treatment, find an oncologist, and even manage the cost of cancer care, which can be almost as devastating as the disease itself.

Diabetes

You *can* be too sweet. Diabetes, a condition of too much sugar in the blood, kills more than 72,000 Americans every year, making it the sixth leading cause of death in the U.S. Here is some information about how to manage this sticky situation.

National Diabetes Information Clearinghouse
diabetes.niddk.nih.gov

The National Diabetes Information Clearinghouse site is a great starting place if you have just been diagnosed with diabetes or if you are trying to keep from getting it. Read tips for controlling your blood sugar through diet, exercise, and, if necessary, insulin.

American Diabetes Association
www.diabetes.org

The American Diabetes Association offers lots of detailed information for managing diabetes through diet and exercise. Find healthy recipes here and tips for fitting fitness into everyday activities. The site also addresses long-term planning—sobering thoughts for those living with a chronic illness.

Alzheimer's Disease

Alzheimer's disease comes in close behind diabetes as the seventh leading cause of death in the U.S. As the population ages, that number may rise. This incurable disease can devastate lives and families. Here are two organizations that do their best to help us cope.

Alzheimer's Association
www.alz.org

The Alzheimer's Association not only features information about the disease (along with a quiz to see if you suffer from it) but also information for caregivers and patients themselves. Visit this

Alzheimer's Association

site to help plan for the changes and challenges that come with Alzheimer's.

Alzheimer's Foundation of America
www.alzfdn.org

This organization addresses the need for long-term care for dementia patients—and how to pay for it. It offers free counseling on this issue via licensed social workers. Write to the foundation through the site or call 866-AFA-8484.

Other Health Organizations

There are hundreds of nonprofit organizations that give informa-tion on all kinds of diseases and conditions. Use these sites to find one that can help with your condition.

Healthfinder.gov: Find a Health Organization

www.healthfinder.gov/findservices/organizations

Browse an alphabetical list of health organizations, and search by health topic or type of organization to find a link to one that suits your situation. This list is sponsored by the U.S. Department of Health and Human Services.

National Organization for Rare Disorders

www.rarediseases.org/search/rdblist.html

If you are one of the unfortunate few who suffer from a rare disease, don't despair! The information that you need can be found at the National Organization for Rare Disorders (NORD) site. Browse the alphabetical list of hundreds of rare diseases to get brief overviews of each, plus links to relevant support organizations.

Mental Health

A troubled mind can't appreciate a healthy body. Use these sites to get your thinking back in the pink.

American Psychological Association: Help Center

www.apa.org/helpcenter

The American Psychological Association offers tips for dealing with a variety of stressors in daily life, including disasters and the threat of terrorism. Try its interactive tool to see how stress affects the whole body. Find a psychologist on this site, and get tips on how to pay for treatment.

Mental Health America: Depression Screening

www.depression-screening.org

Feeling low? Mental Health America offers this confidential depression-screening test along with ten quick tips to help you improve your mood.

TherapistLocator.net

www.aamft.org/therapistlocator

The American Association for Marriage and Family Therapy offers this tool for finding an appropriate counselor in the U.S., Canada, or overseas. The page also offers a selection of articles about mental health issues common among families, such as marital distress and eating disorders.

Finding a Physician

Maybe you need a new doctor because you moved, or you are looking for a specialist, or you just want a second opinion. Find qualified medical professionals with these tools.

American Medical Association: Doctor Finder

www.ama-assn.org/ops/amahg.htm

Use this tool to find basic professional information on virtually every licensed physician in the U.S. Search by name or specialty. You can see where American Medical Association members went to school, the hospitals and health plans they're associated with, and their board certifications. Delve a little deeper by searching on a physician's hospital website, which often provides more details about its doctors.

American Dental Association: Find a Dentist

www.ada.org

Select the Find a Dentist link to search for a qualified dentist in your area.

MedlinePlus: Directories

www.nlm.nih.gov/medlineplus/directories.html

Whether you need a specialist or even a place to donate umbilical cord blood, find a link to the appropriate site with this directory from the National Library of Medicine.

Other Health Tools

Here are a couple of other sites to stash in your home medical kit.

Merriam-Webster Medical Dictionary

www.merriam-webster.com

When I read a medical article, I often don't understand half the words in it. When that happens, I visit the Merriam-Webster Dictionary site. I type in the term I don't know (*adipose tissue*, for example) and then choose the Medical search option. When I click the search button, up pops the definition and a link to hear the word pronounced. Oh! *Adipose tissue* is just a fancy name for my fat pad!

United Hospital Fund: Next Step in Care

nextstepincare.org

As you check out of the hospital, the United Hospital Fund Campaign urges you to use its checklists to keep you from having to go back. This printable list, available in several languages, is especially useful for caregivers. What will be expected of you? Can you take more time off from work to care for your loved one? What do you do if you want to appeal the discharge decision? These issues and more are covered on this comprehensive site.

Lab Tests Online

www.labtestsonline.org

Doctors can tell so much about the state of our health just from blood tests and such. This site gives us laypeople a window to that world of information. Find lab test information by disease, test name, or screening population group. Learn how to interpret the results. Discover which routine test you should undergo and how often.

Medical Apps

Most medical smart phone apps are aimed at professionals. Still, here are two that all of us can use, if we have the right phone for it.

iTunes: WebMD Mobile

itunes.apple.com/app/webmd-mobile/id295076329?mt=8

Use the WebMD Symptom Checker on your iPhone with this free app. Look up drug and treatment information and even get tips on first aid. This would be a great help for an anxious family at the hospital.

Epocrates

www.epocrates.com

This free drug information and pill identification app is meant for medical professionals. Yet patients and caregivers will also find it useful for researching medications. With this mobile app, we can look up our pills even at the pharmacy window. Epocrates is available for Palm, Windows Mobile, iPhone, iPod touch, Android, and BlackBerry.

Drugs

Medications can help us to live long and well. Use these sites to discover what is in your medications and what they do.

PDRhealth: Drug A–Z

www.pdrhealth.com

Explore prescription and over-the-counter medications, along with herbal supplements, in this online version of the *Physicians' Desk Reference*, translated into plain English for consumers.

Check your medications for side effects and interactions with other drugs you may be taking.

RxList: The Internet Drug Index

www.rxlist.com

Search for your prescription medication by name to access its official information, including its chemical structure. Have a loose pill and don't know what it is? Enter its imprint code or even its color and shape into the Pill Identifier wizard.

Clinical Trials

If you are sick with something for which there is no effective standard treatment, you should seriously consider enrolling in an experimental protocol known as a clinical trial. It may be your best hope for a cure or at least a reprieve. And you will be helping to advance medical science at the same time. Here is how to find a clinical trial.

ClinicalTrials.gov

clinicaltrials.gov

The National Institutes of Health (NIH) provide this registry of federal and private clinical trials in the U.S. and other countries. Search by condition and geographical location.

CenterWatch: Clinical Trials

www.centerwatch.com

In contrast to the NIH database, CenterWatch lists research that is being done mostly by the pharmaceutical industry. Find listings for trials involving life-threatening illnesses, as well as for merely troublesome conditions such as sinusitis. The site also lists drugs recently approved by the Food and Drug Administration and links to health organizations for various diseases under Health and Educational Resources.

Quack Attack

When we feel out of control, we are vulnerable to false claims that we would otherwise reject out of hand. Some "medical" websites offer fraudulent or unproven information. Some sites that offer to "find the best doctor" charge for their services. "People in their zeal spend money unnecessarily," notes UCLA librarian Judy Consales.

How can you judge the quality of web health sites? Ask yourself these questions: Who wrote this webpage, and what are his or her credentials? Is the information current and complete enough for your needs? Is the purpose of the site educational, or is it trying to sell me something? You can also look for the seal of approval from the Health On the Net Foundation.

Health On the Net Foundation
www.hon.ch/pat.html

This Geneva, Switzerland-based group guarantees quality of medical webpages with its eight ethical management principles, including the criteria that the site information be supplied by healthcare professionals and that the source of funding for the site is clearly acknowledged. Look for the "HONcode" seal of approval on medical webpages as an assurance of quality. It can mean the difference between finding lifesaving information or bogus nonsense that can cause harm or even death.

Live Long and Prosper

"Men at some time are masters of their fates," Shakespeare wrote. Even though our fate is to eventually pass out of this world, I hope that the health information available on the web can help make the time we have here long and rich. Salud!

17

E-xercise and E-ating Right:
Diet and Fitness on the Web

Women know how it goes. We turn 40, and the tag on our pants that once read "10" now says "16." And the waistband is getting uncomfortably tight.

Not only that, but our email account seems to have taken a note of it. Today, among the offers for male marital aids and three days of personalized psychic service, we will receive at least five bids to help us melt that pad around our middle.

We eat the same way we always have. It seems grossly unfair that we have packed on these pounds.

Medline Plus: Weight Control

www.nlm.nih.gov/medlineplus/weightcontrol.html

According to MedlinePlus from the National Institutes of Health (NIH), apparently we *don't* eat like we used to. In the last 20 years, restaurant portions have grown immensely. Plus, our jobs often keep us sitting in front of computers all day. It's no wonder that two-thirds of Americans are overweight! On this site, the NIH serves up an overview of current thinking on weight control plus an oversized portion of links to quality information about maintaining a healthy body size.

We understand that excess weight causes so many maladies, including diabetes, heart disease, stroke, hypertension, gallbladder disease, osteoarthritis, sleep apnea, and some cancers. Yet, it's hard to resist ads that tell us to consume, brought to us by models who weigh less than 100 pounds. The contradictions are crazy!

Still, that's no reason to reject health and fitness. A healthy body means a healthy brain. To stay sharp, we must exercise and maintain a reasonable weight. The web has tools that can help.

Commercial Weight Control Programs

There are really three ways to approach weight loss. The first is a medical approach, useful if too many pounds immediately threaten one's health. A physician-run program may offer medications or even surgery to help save a patient's life. A second approach is to enroll in commercial programs designed to help us change our lifestyles. The third way is to do it entirely on our own, perhaps with the aid of weight-loss tools on the web.

Several years ago, after I could no longer deny my middle-age weight gain, I chose the second path and joined Weight Watchers.

Weight Watchers
www.weightwatchers.com

Although established in 1962, Weight Watchers has evolved with the times, implementing the latest discoveries in psychology as well as nutrition. The program emphasizes a multifaceted approach to losing weight, including exercising, drinking lots of water, eating nutritious food in smaller portions, maintaining a food journal, and giving lots of positive reinforcement and support. Subscription plans vary, but there is often a registration fee of about $20, followed by weekly dues of about $10. Members who achieve their weight loss goals and keep it going for 6 weeks become "lifetime" members and may attend meetings for free, as long as they stay at their goal weight or lower.

I found the weekly face-to-face meetings surprisingly helpful. I guess it was intellectual arrogance that made me think that I would have little in common with others who struggle with middle-age spread.

For people who cannot attend the meetings, Weight Watchers offers a completely online program featuring instructional newsletters and weekly support in addition to access to online tools like calorie counters. This program runs less than $20 per month if you choose the three-month subscription.

Here are two sites that evaluate commercial weight loss programs, including Weight Watchers.

ConsumerSearch: Weight Loss Programs: Reviews
www.consumersearch.com/weight-loss-programs

To find a quality commercial weight loss program, visit ConsumerSearch's review of reviews. This site compares plans on price as well as short- and long-term effectiveness. See how Weight Watchers stacks up against Slim-Fast or eDiets. ConsumerSearch also tells you what to avoid in a weight loss plan, like fad diets and pills.

Eat Right: Consumer Diet and Lifestyle Book Reviews
www.eatright.org/Media/content.aspx?id=264

Will *Fat Flush for Life* really wash those calories down the drain? Is *The Belly Fat Cure* a true abdominal absolution? Get the pros and cons of the diet-of-the-day from the registered dietitians at the American Dietetic Association.

Self-Help Health and Fitness Sites

It is too bad that just surfing the web doesn't provide enough exercise to lose weight. I'd be a toothpick by now! Still, there are plenty of online resources to help us on our journey. Here is a selection. Choose the one that best suits your style.

MyFitnessPal

www.myfitnesspal.com

Los Angeles actor Alex Egan uses MyFitnessPal to keep trim for his roles. "This site is incredibly simple to use and it's free. You can easily track your calories and exercise. You can instantly find the calorie counts of foods in their database—even name brands and restaurant menu items." Share your goals with your social network with a ticker showing your weight loss progress. Tracking on the go? Download the free app to your iPhone (itunes.apple.com/us/app/calorie-counter-diet-tracker-by/id341232718?mt=8).

BuddySlim

www.buddyslim.com

Want to lose weight in a social environment? "BuddySlim is a great way to get a social support group of people with similar health goals. You make friends that encourage you to stick to your regime and do all your exercises," says Julia Bailey, assistant professor of genetic epidemiology at UCLA. This free site lets users count calories and keep a journal. And, Bailey points out, "since it's over the internet, people don't see each other and judge."

FatSecret

www.fatsecret.com

Here's a full service site that lets you choose your weight and fitness goals and gives you the tools to track your progress. And it's all free. Follow FatSecret's food recommendations, or tie into a commercial diet that you may be following (e.g. Weight Watchers or Atkins). Keep your journal here, and record your calorie intake and exercise. Share your struggles with other members. My favorite part of FatSecret? The free app for my Android smart phone (www.andro lib.com/android.application.com-fatsecret-android-jqpD.aspx) that

BuddySlim

lets me count calories by scanning the barcode on my food packages and then automatically adds them to my food diary online. (Trader Joe's Oatmeal? 170 calories.) There is also a free app for the iPad (itunes.apple.com/us/app/calorie-counter-by-fatsecret/id 364140848?mt=8).

LIVESTRONG.COM's MyPlate

www.livestrong.com/myplate

LIVESTRONG.com offers this site that offers free membership and advice to those who wish to lose weight, manage diabetes, or even cope with bariatric surgery. Track calories eaten and burned during exercise and get support from other members. Download the $2.99 iPhone app to track eating and exercise on the go (itunes.apple.com/us/app/calorie-tracker-achieve-your/id 295305241?mt=8).

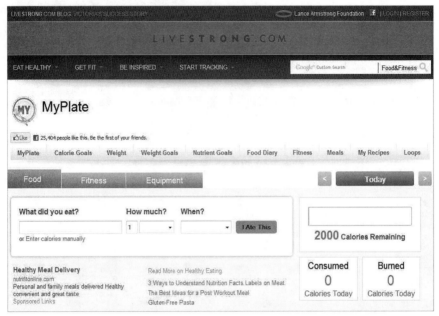

LIVESTRONG.COM's MyPlate

Nutrition

If we want to make our calories count, we've got to know what is in the food that we put in our mouths. Here are tools that let us know what we are eating.

Self: NutritionData

nutritiondata.self.com

This site focuses on food: what to eat and how much. What's your fitness goal and how many calories should you consume to reach it? In return for free registration, members can track their nutritional intake over time. Store the nutritional information for ingredients and recipes here, too.

Food and Drug Administration: Consumer Nutrition and Health Data

www.fda.gov/Food/LabelingNutrition/ConsumerInformation

Sure, I read the nutrition labels on packaged foods. But I don't always understand what they mean. What are the DVs (daily values) versus the %DVs (percent daily values)? Here, the Food and Drug Administration spells it out so that even *I* get it.

USDA Nutrient Database for Standard Reference
www.nal.usda.gov/fnic/cgi-bin/nut_search.pl

Here's a federal site for serious nutrition wonks. Do you really want to know how much manganese is in the average celery stick? Well, let's just say that carrots contain a lot more. Browse the nutrient list to view reports on foods by single nutrients (e.g., the aforementioned manganese), or do a keyword search.

General Advice About Food and Health

Learning to change our lifestyles is a complicated process. Here is a selection of sites that offer support in a variety of ways.

WebMD: Healthy Eating & Diet
www.webmd.com/diet

WebMD serves up this cornucopia of information about healthy eating and fitness. Read the latest news and advice about diets. Use the site tools to find your BMI (body mass index), a personal assessment of your diet, and a food and fitness planner. Check the Food-o-Meter to see the nutritional information of more than 37,000 foods.

Hungry Girl
www.hungry-girl.com

This is a fun Weight Watchers tie-in site with lots of advice about recipes and restaurant dining. Lisa Lillien is the real name of the girl. Follow her on this site or on Facebook (www.facebook.com/HungryGirl) or Twitter.

WebMD: Healthy Eating & Diet

Eat This, Not That

eatthis.menshealth.com or eatthis.womenshealthmag.com

In their book, *Eat This, Not That! Thousands of Simple Food Swaps That Can Save You 10, 20, 30 Pounds—or More!* (Rodale, 2007), David Zinczenko and Matt Goulding compare similar foods with wildly different nutritional content. On this site, they compare restaurant offerings and suggest that, if we make the right choices, we can shed pounds without actually having to count calories. Browse national restaurant chains by name or food type to see their overall grades for a healthy, nutritious menu (e.g., Au Bon Pain: A-; Applebee's: F). There are nutrition tips here, too, along with a "Menu Decoder" to help us figure out what are the best choices while eating out.

American Heart Association and American Stroke Association: My Life Check

mylifecheck.heart.org

How's your overall health, and how can you tweak your lifestyle to improve it? The American Heart Association, along with the American Stroke Association, offers this tool to help you see where you stand in seven major areas including weight and physical activity. Tip: Have your blood pressure and cholesterol numbers at the ready.

Overeaters Anonymous

www.oa.org

Overeaters Anonymous (OA) offers a program of recovery from compulsive overeating using the Twelve Steps and Twelve Traditions of OA. As it approaches overeating as a behavioral disorder, it does not endorse a specific diet or fitness plan. Instead, it addresses physical, emotional, and spiritual well-being.

Mayo Clinic: Levine Lab—NEAT

mayoresearch.mayo.edu/mayo/research/levine_lab

What if you could lose weight just by walking around the office? James A. Levine directs the lab at Mayo Clinic that studies "non-exercise activity thermogenesis" or NEAT. NEAT involves the energy that we expend while performing the activities of our everyday life, apart from formal exercise. Levine found that people can comfortably work at computers while walking on a treadmill going about 1 mile per hour. At that pace, they can burn 100 calories every hour, enough to lose 50 pounds in a year. Although such treadmill workstations are not commercially available, many people have fashioned them and put their plans on the web. Build your own (www.treadmill-desk.com).

Exercise

Recently, 460 surviving participants of the Scottish Mental Survey of 1932 were tested, at age 79, on the same general cognitive test that they took at age 11. The results were surprising.

Overwhelmingly, the strongest correlation to the preservation of IQ after 68 years was physical fitness.

Physical fitness! Not violin lessons, not brain teasers. Only keeping the body moving kept the mind sharp. It appears that a healthy brain is linked to a strong heart and circulatory system, and physical activity promotes this essential cardiac fitness.

So it's not just a matter of losing weight. We've got to work out to keep from losing our marbles! Here's help.

About.com: Exercise
exercise.about.com

Certified personal trainer Paige Waehner is the About.com guide to exercise. She writes, "It is difficult to stay motivated to exercise, but the internet is an excellent source for information and support. Through my site, you can access the best websites, weekly exercise articles, and a community dedicated to helping you stay in shape." This terrific portal features a "Workout Center," a directory of links to all kinds of exercise info, and a section called "Exercise for Beginners" for those who are just getting started.

Fitness.com
www.fitness.com/exercises

Canada's Fitness.com shows us how to do more than 300 exercises. A free registration gives users a place to plan and track exercise, forums for discussing fitness, and access to videos illustrating proper exercise technique, including workouts that can be done in an office setting.

FitTracker
fittracker.shapefit.com

Guys, do you need exercise? Come here for exercise instruction and fitness tracking tools. Register for free to track the change in your biceps, chest, and thighs as you complete levels of training.

Of course, women can use this site, too. Still, the excellent exercise descriptions and animations seem oriented toward bodybuilding gentlemen.

Diet and Fitness Apps

Smart phone owners can help themselves from a heaping smorgasbord of diet and fitness apps. Whet your appetite with this tiny sample.

iTunes: Lose It!

itunes.apple.com/app/lose-it/id297368629?mt=8

FitNow provides this free iPhone app for tracking calorie intake and exercise. Set your daily "budget" of calories. Lose It helps you watch your waist by watching your "spending."

iTunes: Weightbot

itunes.apple.com/app/id293642937?mt=8

This adorable $1.99 iPhone app lets users track their weight on a pretty interface. The data is backed up online at the Weightbot website (weightbot.com).

CardioTrainer

www.worksmartlabs.com/cardiotrainer/about.php

Download the free CardioTrainer to your GPS-enabled Android smart phone. As long as the phone is with you as you exercise, the app will track your movement and calculate your burn. Log in to the website to see your overall history. The program can also feed into Facebook to share your workout progress with all your friends.

Some Success

After being on Weight Watchers for about 6 months, I lost about 10 percent of my starting weight. I went down two sizes and looked a lot better! I made some permanent lifestyle changes that stayed with me through the years.

During that time, when my husband dressed for work, he had to punch new notches in his belt and gather his pants in folds around his waist. Because of my diet, he lost 25 pounds! Not exactly fair, is it?

18

Tech Support:
Self-Help and Support Groups

We would rather be ruined than changed;
We would rather die in our dread
Than climb the cross of the moment
And let our illusions die.

—W. H. Auden

I have a friend, I'll call her "Pat," who has a drinking problem. When she told me about it, I was surprised. She never misses work and seems fairly cheerful. Still, she confessed that over the last few years, her drinking had gotten out of control. "First, I drank to feel better," she reported, "but then I got to the point that I had to drink to stop the cravings that were driving me crazy."

Pat was seeing a psychiatrist to help curb her addiction. He had prescribed Wellbutrin, an anti-depressant that, under the name Zyban, is also used to curb nicotine cravings, and Campral, a medication recently approved by the Food and Drug Administration to ease alcohol withdrawal symptoms. The doctor also suggested that she attend Alcoholics Anonymous (AA) meetings to support her during her life change.

She resisted. "I felt that I had to find the strength within myself to quit drinking. The last thing I needed was to say that I was powerless over my problem," Pat declared. Still, she agreed to research other programs that she could use to help her change her bad habit.

She came across the Women for Sobriety website and sent for some materials. When they arrived, she told me, "I was so surprised by the positive approach of the program that I stopped drinking then and there."

Women for Sobriety, Inc.

www.womenforsobriety.org

This Pennsylvania-based woman's group was started in 1975 by Jean Kirkpatrick, a sociologist who achieved sobriety by reading Emerson and other metaphysical writers. She believed that women alcoholics had specific emotional needs not addressed by AA: depression, low self-esteem, excessive guilt, and loneliness.

From her reading, Kirkpatrick distilled thirteen "statements of acceptance" that women can use to build a new self-image and feel strong enough to overcome their need for alcohol and other drugs. These statements include an acknowledgment of the problem, a dismissal of the past, and pledges to practice happiness and enthusiasm in the service of emotional and spiritual growth. Members are encouraged to visualize themselves as competent and capable, ready and able to handle life's difficulties without the need of addictive chemicals.

Participants may meet in person and also join in moderated online discussion sessions and chat. Here, they encourage each other, share and applaud successes, and swap tips for countering urges to return to their old lifestyle. Although the Women for Sobriety program differs from AA, it does not contradict it, and many women belong to both groups.

"I haven't had a glass of wine since I joined the program several years ago," Pat exclaimed in amazement. "I can't believe it! I feel so much support from the ladies in the program."

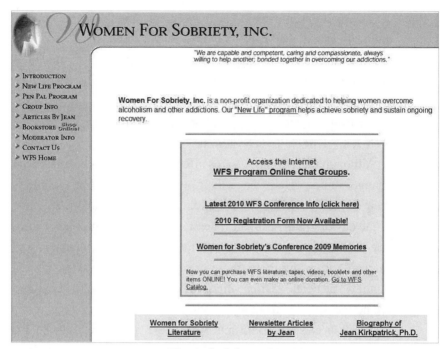

Women for Sobriety, Inc.

Way to go, Pat! Sounds like Women for Sobriety is an almost fun way to solve a serious life problem.

We all have something that we would like to change about ourselves. Many of us are sedentary; we could use some exercise. The frustrations and anxieties of life could drive any of us to overdrink. If we smoke … well, we've got to stop that, right now.

There are so many bad habits, both overwhelming and trivial, that we may want to change, as well as positive habits that we may want to embrace, such as exercise or investing. Although we may turn to health professionals for assistance in altering our behaviors, many of us will use self-help groups to help achieve positive change in our lives.

The modern self-help movement began in the 1930s with the founding of AA. The peer-support movement really took off in the

1970s when the concept of "empowerment" and the questioning of authority established itself in the American zeitgeist.

When the web appeared, it proved perfectly suited to the loose structure of these peer-support groups. Today, there are advice sites, discussion boards, and chat rooms for every kind of difficulty, from anxiety to support for wives and girlfriends of men with XXY Klinefelter's Syndrome.

Although face-to-face groups offer a strong support for personal change, online groups have their advantages. The biggest one is their eternal availability; inspiration is only a click away, any time of the day or night. Also, these sessions have no geographic boundaries. "I read messages from women in Australia, Canada, and England, in addition to those from women across the United States," Pat notes. "Often, these ladies live in places where there are no face-to-face meetings of Women for Sobriety."

These peer-support forums work best as general advice for chronic conditions that are not life-threatening in the short-term. Users should not rely on information exchanged in chat rooms and discussion boards as a replacement for qualified medical advice. Those who feel suicidal or who are in immediate danger should pick up a telephone and call 911.

Support Group Directories

Most self-help groups focus on health problems, both physical and mental. Often, a national advocacy organization for a particular condition will host discussion boards where sufferers can ask questions and share advice.

As you consider signing up for online support groups, you might also want to establish a new, anonymous free email account to use on these sites. Information in cyberspace is remarkably persistent and may be discovered by employers and insurers—or scam artists. AA takes pains to ensure the privacy of its members; participants in online peer support may want to do the same.

Here are websites that list a variety of online health discussion groups.

WebMD Health Exchange

exchanges.webmd.com

The WebMD message boards are a good place to share information about specific diseases and conditions. Do an alphabetical or keyword search, or browse through the directory structure of health topics. Some of these are moderated by WebMD staff and health experts; others are created and monitored by users. Free registration is required for posting.

iVillage Message Boards

forums.ivillage.com

Women can register for free to access more than 1,000 message boards with subjects ranging from decorating to romance to health issues, such as quitting smoking and coping with cancer.

DailyStrength

www.dailystrength.org

Members register for free to gain access to discussion sites for more than 500 diseases and conditions including insomnia, eating disorders, sensory integration disorders, and "parenting teenagers." Sufferers can keep an online journal or blog; caregivers, friends, and strangers can offer support and even virtual hugs. Most of the support groups are unmoderated, although members may ask a question of the site's health experts.

American Self-Help Group Clearinghouse:
Self-Help Group Sourcebook Online

mentalhelp.net/selfhelp

Do a keyword search in this comprehensive database to find links to mental and physical self-help groups. Many of these organizations sponsor chats and discussion boards.

12-Step Recovery Support Groups and Resources

Since 1935, Americans have weaned themselves off of alcohol with the help of the 12 steps from AA. This organization has served as a model for peer-support organizations that wish to wean users from other harmful addictions. Today, whatever your "poison," a 12-step support group can help you get off it. Examples include Gamblers Anonymous, Emotions Anonymous, Narcotics Anonymous, Sexaholics Anonymous, Overeaters Anonymous, and Alateen.

The following are online support groups and resources based on the 12-step program for recovery. Some are just for alcohol, while others cover a range of addictions.

In the Rooms
intherooms.com

Most support groups encourage anonymity. In the Rooms takes the opposite tack, encouraging members to share their journey of 12-step recovery with friends on Facebook. The site features a general chat room, discussion sites devoted to the various official 12-step "fellowships," forums, and member-created groups. The site also offers links to in-person treatment programs. Works on mobile web browsers, too.

Miracles In Progress: 12-Step Recovery Forums
www.12stepforums.net

Miracles In Progress 12-Step Recovery Forums feature continuous support for members of AA, Narcotics Anonymous, Childhood Abuse Survivors, and a teen and family forum. Attend real-time meetings in Java-based chat, or post and answer questions on the message boards.

IN THE ROOMS®, you can Find Old Friends,

Make New Friends, Seek Help in Recovery,

Create a Group, Learn about Recovery,

Choose Your Level of Privacy,

and much more...

"The best thing about ITR is that they don't endorse any particular fellowship or form of treatment. They understand that the point is to get clean and stay clean."

--Leyva

In the Rooms

StepChat

stepchat.com

Recovery Chat Rooms feature 12-step meetings and open fellowship chat. The site requires free registration.

SoberRecovery: Alcoholism Drug Addiction
Help and Information

www.soberrecovery.com/forums

Join for free and participate in online forums aimed at various segments of the substance abuse community.

The Recovery Group

www.therecoverygroup.org

Those who wish 12-step support for overeating issues can chat on this Java-based chat room any time—literally.

Alcoholics Anonymous

www.aa.org

Here is the home page of the original self-help recovery group. Visit the site to learn about alcoholism and the possibility of recovery via the 12 steps. The full text of the "Big Book" by AA founder Bill W. is here (www.aa.org/bbonline) along with AAGrapevine. org (www.aagrapevine.org), the official online publication of Alcoholics Anonymous International. The print version of this journal, referred to as the "meeting in print," has been published since 1944.

iTunes: 12 Steps AA Companion

itunes.apple.com/us/app/12-steps-aa-companion-alcoholics /id295775656?mt=8

Yes, there's an app for this! Download this $2.99 app to your iPhone to track your journey to recovery through the 12 steps of AA.

Alternatives to AA

It has been said that the AA program, with its emphasis on reliance upon God and public confession and redemption, is popular with Americans because we are, in general, a religious people, living in a nation founded by Calvinists.

Still, there are those for whom the 12-step program is too religious, too focused on the problem and not the solution, or simply not based on scientific principles. Programs for these folks are harder to find, particularly in the physical world. Fortunately, alternatives are just a click away in cyberspace. Women for Sobriety is one. Here are others.

SMART Recovery

smartrecovery.org

Billing itself as an "alternative to Alcoholics Anonymous and Narcotics Anonymous," SMART (Self-Management And Recovery Training) Recovery is a clinically proven program to help people overcome addictions of all kinds. It sponsors meetings around the world as well as offering free meetings and message boards online.

SOS: Save Our Selves

www.sossobriety.org

Secular Organizations for Sobriety, or Save Our Selves, was organized in 1985 by Los Angeles writer James Christopher as a secular alternative to the religion inherent in the 12-step programs. SOS meetings are anonymous and free and stress Christopher's "Sobriety Priority" theory of abstinence-based self-empowerment. Explore its online discussion groups on Yahoo! Groups (health.groups.yahoo.com/group/sossaveourselves).

Moderation Management

www.moderation.org

Participants of Moderation Management abstain from drinking for 30 days, then keep close tabs on their consumption so that they can meet their goals of abstinence or moderation. Members may meet in person, join a listserv, or participate in online chat.

Online Support for Other Physical and Mental Conditions

In addition to substance abuse, other chronic conditions also respond well to support, either in person or online, from a group of fellow sufferers. Here is a grab bag of quality sites.

QuitNet: Quit Smoking All Together

www.quitnet.com

So you want to quit smoking? Make this difficult life change with help from others. A free QuitNet membership gives access to basic smoking cessation information and support, both from the site and from fellow quitters. Premium members, who pay about 10 bucks per month, receive personalized advice and a place for an online journal. This site was originally developed by the Boston University School of Public Health.

H-C: Compulsive Hoarding Community

health.groups.yahoo.com/group/H-C

This online support group is run and moderated by professionals from the International OCD Foundation (www.ocfoundation. org). Yahoo! Groups host a variety of OCD (obsessive compulsive disorder) support boards (health.groups.yahoo.com/group/OCD SupportGroups/links).

QuitNet: Quit Smoking All Together

Pink-Link

www.pink-link.org

"Cancer is a club you didn't ask to join," says this site. Breast cancer survivors can join for free to share resources and advice.

Spine-Health: Back Pain, Back Surgery, and
Pain Problem Message Boards

www.spine-health.com/forum

Back pain sufferers, register here to participate in active exchange forums for those with aching spines.

American Diabetes Association Message Boards

connect.diabetes.org/forums

Get answers and find consolation among others who share your condition. Twelve discussion groups are aimed at a variety of users: teens, parents of children with diabetes, those with gestational diabetes, and adults with Type 1 or Type 2 versions of the disease. There is a Spanish-language discussion group, too, called "Esquina de la Diabetes." You must register if you want to post to the site, but registration is free.

dLife: Diabetes Support Forum

www.dlife.com/diabetes-forum

Here's another site where diabetics can get advice from nurses and fellow sufferers.

The Six Stages of Change

Successful self-changers always go through several specific stages of change, according to the book, *Changing for Good* (Collins; Reprint edition, 1995) by psychologists James O. Prochaska, John C. Norcross, and Carlo C. DiClemente. If we understand these stages, we can manage them to achieve change more efficiently:

- The first stage is "precontemplation," in which people with problems defensively refuse to acknowledge them and tend to blame others for their difficulties. In alcoholics, this stage is popularly referred to as "denial."

- In the second stage, sufferers begin to question their habits and begin to learn about how to change them. This is the "contemplation" period.

- "Preparation" is the third short stage, in which subjects make small changes and set a date in the near future to finally take …

- "Action," the fourth stage. In the action stage, self-changers make the jump and either stop a bad habit or take up a good one.

- After the excitement of action comes the "maintenance" stage, with its difficult task of solidifying a new behavior.

- Finally, after 2–3 years, changers may enter "termination," the final stage of change, in which the formerly troublesome habit no longer offers temptation under any circumstances.

Most self-changers cycle through contemplation, preparation, action, and maintenance several times before finally cementing a positive change. Called the "Spiral of Change," these attempts are never wasted, because lessons learned can be used in "recycling" once again through the stages of change.

All Better Now?

These are only a few of the free peer-support groups on the web that are available for almost any trouble one can think to share. Here's hoping that these groups will help someone in your life overcome a difficulty that has been bothering them for a long time!

19

Latency:
Help for Procrastination and Productivity

It has been my good fortune to have a gig writing a column for *Searcher* magazine, a trade publication for librarians. Every month, when I once again sit down in front of a blank page in Microsoft Word, a thought or an image scuttles across my frontal lobe just behind my eyes: my bathtub … with footprints in it. Suddenly, I am gripped with the urge to scrub every inch of dingy tile, a chore I have managed to avoid for more than 3 weeks.

My house is never so clean as when I am writing at home. On the other hand, the brilliant white of the bathtub tile now recalls to mind the shining white emptiness of that Word page. Sigh.

This is a behavioral pattern that I have enacted all of my adult life. When faced with a task that I do not particularly want to start, I feel compelled to take care of old business—jobs that I had previously put off. Every time I do it, I feel guilty and even more anxious about the work at hand. It's torture. My editor Barbara Quint refers to this particular form of behavior as "working procrastination." She claims it's how she gets all her ideas for the articles in the issues she's not supposed to be working on. In response to this rationalization, I say, "Whatever gets you through the night."

251

"Age quod agis" admonishes the Latin motto: "Do what you are doing." Wise words, at home and on the job, but difficult for me to follow. Judging from the overwhelming amount of "productivity" advice and merchandise available on the web, I sense that I am not alone. Procrastination, it seems, is a problem intrinsic to human nature.

Let's waste a little time exploring a few of these web resources to see if they can help us work more efficiently and with less angst.

Productivity Systems

Just as there are fads in dieting, so too are there timely trends for productivity philosophies and tools. Here are some current ones.

David Allen: Getting Things Done

www.davidco.com

The most popular productivity philosophy of the moment is David Allen's Getting Things Done, or GTD. Based on Allen's 2001 book, *Getting Things Done: The Art of Stress-Free Productivity* (Viking Adult), the method advocates recording and sorting to-do lists. (You know, the ones that float around in your head and make you crazy ... unless they disappear completely.) The method dictates that complex tasks should be broken down into small, doable bits. We should dispatch things that can be done in less than 2 minutes immediately. We must write down our ideas, not try to keep them in our heads. This should impart a sense of calm, a "mind like water," which is an effective state in which to solve problems.

Allen has the soul of a super library cataloger. If only we could categorize our tasks properly, he seems to say, they would practically complete themselves. Such a system would be ideal to keep complex operations on schedule. Although this procrastinatrix resists the idea of applying so much structure to my piddling projects, I could make myself more productive if I adopted some GTD tactics. Perhaps I should give myself a leg up by purchasing some of the books, software, and notebooks available on Allen's site. More likely, I'll catch his articles on the Huffington Post (www.huffingtonpost.com/david-allen).

FranklinCovey

www.franklincovey.com

A slightly older but still fantastically popular time management philosophy comes from Stephen R. Covey and his 1989 book, *The Seven Habits of Highly Effective People* (Simon & Schuster). Covey's principles encourage followers to become proactively responsible for solving problems and then to work in a way that benefits all involved in a job. Like Allen, Covey emphasizes the importance of organizing a project before jumping in to work on it and confirms the utility of a clear goal or vision. Download the FCmobilelife Tasks app for iPhone for about $6 (www.fcmobile life.com/products/fctasks.php).

Action Method Online

www.actionmethod.com

Manhattan's Scott Belsky and his team have developed this web-based project management system that can serve one or many. It can help individuals break down projects into those doable steps. Its strong social networking aspect allows managers to assign tasks to subordinates and even to "nag" them. The service is free for limited use; $99 buys a year of unlimited organizational fun. There is even a free iPhone app for organizing on the run (www.action method.com/iPhone_Tour).

Productivity Blogs

The systems just mentioned may show the broad outlines of how to get organized, but plenty of blogs out there fill in the details of putting these systems into action. Here is a sampling.

Lifehacker: Top 10 Motivation Boosters and Procrastination Killers

lifehacker.com/5533897/top-10-motivation-boosters-and-procrastination-killers

This blog is like having a super-smart friend with excellent answers for practical life questions. Here, it presents 10 strong ideas for boosting productivity and subduing procrastination. Tips include "Use Minor Distractions to Fend Off Big Distractions" and "Set a Timer and Crank Until It Beeps."

43 Folders

www.43folders.com

"43 folders" refers to the GTD technique of keeping a "tickler" file of things to do in file folders: one for every day of the month (31 max) and every month of the year (12). As the month passes, the contents of the daily folders go into your inbox. The empty day folders move on into next month's queue. San Francisco's Merlin Mann writes about this and other GTD techniques to help us find the time and attention to do our best work.

43 Folders

Productivity501

www.productivity501.com

Since September 2005, consultant Mark W. Shead has published weekly tips about how to improve personal productivity. Snag his column with your feed reader or browse his articles by date or general category. Shead also offers a free 10-day email course about how to overcome procrastination. He even sells ambient sound files to help cut out distractions and focus the brain.

GigaOM: WebWorkerDaily

gigaom.com/collaboration

Find GTD tips here along with many other ideas about how to become productive while working from home.

LifeDev

lifedev.net

LifeDev offers GTD advice to "empower creative people."

Getting Things Done: My Experiences With Using GTD

gtd.marvelz.com/blog

This is hardcore GTD: all productivity all the time. Buy GTD books, software, and worksheets here too.

The Problem of Distraction

We might increase our productivity if we could only reduce the distractions that keep us from concentrating. Here is some help for that.

Psychology Today: Multitasking—Efficient or a Waste of Time?

www.psychologytoday.com/blog/crisis-center/200809/
multitasking-efficient-or-waste-time

Remember when doing several things at once was considered a great way to get things done? Turns out, the opposite is true. Forensic psychologist John A. Call explains how the brain can only focus on one thing at a time. It takes time and energy to switch it to a new task. "Navigating these two stages within your brain can actually take up as much as 40% of your productive time." Who knew?

The New Atlantis: The Myth of Multitasking
www.thenewatlantis.com/publications/the-myth-of-multitasking

Christine Rosen, senior editor at *The New Atlantis* magazine, summarizes recent findings that prove multitasking is a production killer.

FlyLady.net: How to Declutter
flylady.net/pages/FLYingLessons_Declutter.asp

Clutter can be a big distraction in the workspace! FlyLady Marla Cilley offers tips for super-fast and effective ways to de-clutter. However, Cilley emphasizes that we must not work too long at any one time to remove clutter. Instead, every day, set a timer for 15 minutes and work like fury!

How to Declutter

Taking 15 minutes each day to declutter an area, using the 27-Fling Boogie, and clearing your hotspots are among some of the most powerful tools you can use to create a more peaceful home. Remember: You cannot organize clutter - you can only organize the things you love!

I've included my tips on how to declutter. Put your home on a diet. If this is difficult for you, try reading one of my favorite books, "Clear Your Clutter with Feng Shui" by Karen Kingston.

1. **When to Declutter:** Decide how often you are going to declutter a zone. Do a little every day - use a timer. But be warned - this can become compulsive! Once you get started you will want to clean like a banshee! Don't burn yourself out! Only do small amount at a time. The house did not get dirty overnight and it will not get clean overnight. When you set the timer you can only do two sessions at a time. This goal may seem unattainable right now, but you can do it in little pieces. In a couple of months, the whole house will be decluttered.

2. **Decluttering Equipment:** You will need garbage bags, boxes, magic markers, and a dust rag. Label the boxes "Give Away", "Throw Away", and "Put Away". Line the "Throw Away" box with a plastic garbage bag.

3. **Set your timer:** for 1 hour (or 30, 15, or 10 minutes - it doesn't matter how long). Just do the job as fast as you can and do not pull out more stuff than you can put away in that length of time. This means just one drawer, one closet (or even one shelf in one closet), one magazine rack, or digging under just the furniture in the zone. Not all of them at once!

© 2001 FlyLady All Rights Reserved
Home
Shop our Store
Search

FlyLady.net: How to Declutter

The Clutter Control Rules

www.thecleanteam.com/rules-clutter

Jeff Campbell shares his 13 rules for getting rid of clutter. My favorite, and the one that I always forget, is "Handle something once." Whenever you bring something into the house, do not put it down until it reaches its proper place, either in appropriate storage or the recycling bin. Come to think of it, Campbell's rules for banishing clutter sound a lot like Allen's rules for getting things done!

The Problem of Procrastination

In the end, it doesn't matter how organized or neat we are if we still refuse to do the things that we are supposed to. Procrastinators do not have a problem with time management; they have much more complex issues with self-regulation, according to Joseph Ferrari, PhD, associate professor of psychology at De Paul University in Chicago.

Sounds serious, but there's got to be some way around it. Here are some tips.

Psychology Today: Procrastination—
10 Things You Should Know

www.psychologytoday.com/articles/200308/procrastination
-ten-things-know

After consultation with psychological experts, Hara Estroff Marano delineates the big problems with chronic procrastination, including the fact that society does not take the problem seriously enough and the difficulty in treating it.

Psychology Today: Don't Delay

blogs.psychologytoday.com/blog/dont-delay

Timothy Pychyl, professor of psychology at Carleton University in Ottawa and an expert on procrastination behavior, writes this blog to provide the psychological know-how needed to overcome our tendency to put things off. Three big tips: 1) Just get started;

BLOGS
Don't Delay
Understanding procrastination and how to achieve our goals.
by Timothy A. Pychyl

The Procrastinator's Digest: My new book is now available

My sabbatical ended June 30th. It was a wonderful year for reading and writing. Among my writing projects was a short book - *The Procrastinator's Digest: A Concise Guide to Solving the Procrastination Puzzle*. This blog post includes the introductory chapter of the book. It provides an overview of my approach and what you can expect. Read More

2 more tips for Beating Writer's Block

When I see something about writer's block, I immediately think of Robert Boice's work on procrastination and blocking. He has also written an excellent book about new faculty. Here are two more strategies to add to Bill Knaus' list of tips based on Boice's research. Read More

Procrastination can make you happy?

Does procrastination make us happy? Does it improve performance? The short answer from the accumulated research literature is "no" on both accounts. So, why does this myth persist? Read More

Psychology Today: Don't Delay

2) Don't expect to feel good (at least at first); and 3) "Be honest with yourself." Oh wait now, there's the problem …

CalPoly: Study Library Skills—Procrastination
sas.calpoly.edu/asc/ssl/procrastination.html

California Polytechnic State University at San Luis Obispo, California, offers salient tips to help students (and all of us) understand and overcome procrastination.

The Ultimate Goal

Why do we try to be more productive at work? Is it to relieve the anxiety of avoidance? Or are we just giving "the Man" more bang for his personnel buck?

In September 2007, Carnegie Mellon professor Randy Pausch, then outwardly hale and hearty, spoke about his life and imminent death; he would pass away from pancreatic cancer 10 months later ("Achieving Your Childhood Dreams," www.youtube.com/watch?v=ji5_MqicxSo). He wanted us all to know that time is our most precious commodity and that the best reason to save time at work is to increase the amount of it we have to share with the people we love.

Pausch died on July 25, 2008, leaving behind a wife and three young children. He knew that the memories of the time he spent with them would be his most precious legacy. He prioritized his time with this rule: "If I do X, will it matter? And if I have to pick either X or Y, which one is more important? At the end of my life, which of these things will I be glad I did?"

He may have been on to something.

20

E-Lation:
Using the Web to Feel Happier

Many of us are not depressed, yet we live with a nagging feeling that life is kind of blah. We wish that we could be happier. But how can we make that happen? Would more money make us happier? A better relationship? Not having so many aches and pains?

Sonja Lyubomirsky, psychology professor at the University of California at Riverside, cites recent research showing that, although these good things can make us happy for a little while, the effect doesn't last (*The How of Happiness: A Scientific Approach to Getting the Life You Want*, Penguin Press, 2007). Persistent happiness comes from within. We create it for ourselves, by spending time with friends, getting in daily exercise or physical activity, feeling grateful for what we have, and having a sense of purpose in life.

That's a fine prescription for normal everyday ennui, but what about when something really bad happens? For example, large numbers of people were laid off in this last recession. For many of us, losing a job would be a personal catastrophe. It not only means the end of a salary and health benefits (if we had them) but also possibly a loss of identity. We humans are social creatures. To flourish, we require secure roles in communities: in families and social groups—and in our workplaces. Particularly in the U.S, we take our identity from our work. Surely losing a job is a legitimate reason for unhappiness.

TED: Dan Gilbert Asks, Why Are We Happy?
www.ted.com/index.php/talks/dan_gilbert_asks_why_are
_we_happy.html

In this video from TED, Harvard psychologist Dan Gilbert explains how our prefrontal cortex predicts (mostly incorrectly) what will make us happy. We perceive that our happiness comes from outside of ourselves, but research shows that we actually synthesize our own happiness. When bad things happen that we can't control, our "psychological immune system" kicks in and rationalizes the outcome to make it seem to our advantage. If we are aware of this propitious reaction, we can make it kick in faster when adversity strikes. (By the way, TED stands for "Technology, Entertainment, Design." It began in 1984 as a conference bringing together people from those three worlds. Now, fascinating presentations from its yearly gatherings are available for free online.)

It's great to know that we have a psychological immune system that can help us bounce back from disaster. But how does it work?

In his book *Transitions: Making Sense of Life's Changes* (2nd edition, Da Capo Press, 2004), William Bridges offers a framework for the navigation of life shifts, such as job loss, that shake our very foundations. In addition to outward changes, he says we undergo interior transitions in three stages: "endings," a "neutral zone," and finally "beginnings," the time in which we assume our new identity.

Bridges emphasizes the importance of acknowledging endings: the "de-identification" of ourselves from our former roles. It is also critical that we allow ourselves to fully experience the neutral zone, a fallow period before something new can start. Bridges says that we should use this confusing and distressing time for reassessment and creativity. After the endings and neutral zone phases play themselves out, we can joyously embrace our new beginnings.

A recent review article demonstrates that happy people are more successful than sad ones.[1] Given that fact, it's a good idea to work on improving our mood as we reconcile our endings and tolerate the neutral zones of change. Perhaps the web can help.

Psychological Tests

How are we feeling today? The first step is to take some psychological tests to find out.

Psychology Today: Test Yourself

www.psychologytoday.com/tests

Got nothing but time … time to learn about yourself? Take one of these 76 professionally developed, free psychological quizzes to explore your own attitudes toward relationships, health, and career. Assess your IQ. And also find out how happy you are with your life.

BBC News: Test Your Happiness

news.bbc.co.uk/2/hi/programmes/happiness_formula/4785402.stm

Professor Ed Diener from the University of Illinois designed this short test designed to measure your current level of happiness.

Signal Patterns

www.signalpatterns.com

Here's psychological assessment for the Web 2.0 generation! Sign up for free to take the personality, music preference, and parenting style surveys, and then show the results on Facebook and other social networks and blogs. Signal Patterns also sells positive psychology iPhone apps for tracking gratitude (free), assessing your personality ($.99), parenting tendencies (free), and detecting career orientation (free). Fans of Deepak Chopra can de-stress using his six-week $2.99 iPhone course or his $1.99 yoga app.

Psychology Today: Test Yourself

Finally, the $.99 Live Happy app can remind iPhone owners how to feel better during the day.

University of Pennsylvania Authentic Happiness Questionnaires Center

www.authentichappiness.sas.upenn.edu/questionnaires.aspx

Martin Seligman, the founder of the Positive Psychology movement, offers 19 surveys on this site in return for free registration. Measure today's happiness and your characteristic level of satisfaction. Do you find meaning in your life? Do you have grit and perseverance? The results can serve as clues for your next life moves.

The How of Happiness

There has been a lot of work in recent years concerning positive psychology, the study of what humans need to be happy. Here are some sites that discuss it.

BBC News: The Science of Happiness

news.bbc.co.uk/2/hi/programmes/happiness_formula/4783836.stm

Mike Rudin, producer of the BBC program *The Happiness Formula*, explains how happiness makes us healthier and longer-lived. He outlines the basic ingredients of happiness, including strong relationships and a sense of meaning in life.

PsyBlog: 18 Ways Attention Goes Wrong

www.spring.org.uk/2009/04/18-ways-attention-goes-wrong.php

We know that some people have a hard time paying attention. But what if depression and anxiety were the result of paying too much attention? This article explores the idea that problems with attention balance underlie many of our psychological ills.

VIA Survey of Character: Learn What's Best About You

www.viacharacter.org/SURVEYS.aspx

We all have weaknesses. What would happen if we forgot about those and just paid attention to our character strengths instead? Take this 240-question survey, developed by Chris Peterson, professor at the University of Michigan, to find your most competent characteristics. The test and a brief report is free in return for registration. In-depth analysis of your strengths is available for $40.

PsyBlog: How to Choose Happiness—Combat 5 Decision-Making Biases

www.spring.org.uk/2008/05/how-to-choose-happiness-combat-5.php

We are trapped in our present emotions and can't really make decisions based on a future emotional state. Furthermore, we overestimate what we imagine will be the impact of future events. We also make decisions based on our (necessarily) selective memories. With our faulty brains, it's amazing that we ever make a proper choice!

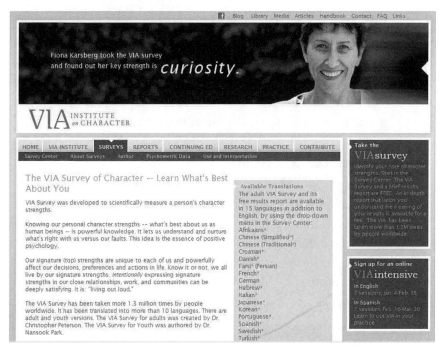

VIA Survey of Character: Learn What's Best About You

Good Radio Shows, Inc. and Peace Talks Radio:
The Neuroscience of Compassion

www.goodradioshows.org/peaceTalksL61.htm

In this excerpt from a radio interview, Richard J. Davidson, psychology professor at the University of Wisconsin-Madison, explains the connection between the amygdala, the part of our brain responsible for fearful reactions, and our frontal cortex, which can resonate with the amygdala or alternately, can calm it down.

Instant Relief

All the advice is terrific and wonderful to implement over time. But what can we do to feel better right now?

Harvard Health Publications: Your Portable Guide to Stress Relief

www.health.harvard.edu/PDFs/Stress_Relief_Guide.pdf

Follow these few suggestions from Harvard Medical School to help alleviate stress. Ideas include reaching out to others, correcting negative assumptions, and learning physical relaxation techniques that you can practice on the go.

The Happiness Project: Eight Tips for Making Yourself Happier in the Next Hour

www.happiness-project.com/happiness_project/2008/06/eight-tips-for.html

Gretchen Rubin, a former lawyer, spent a year looking for happiness by "test-driving every principle, tip, theory, and scientific study [she] could find, whether from Aristotle or St. Therese or Martin Seligman or Oprah." She writes about her findings on her blog and in her book, *The Happiness Project: Or, Why I Spent a Year Trying to Sing in the Morning, Clean My Closets, Fight Right, Read Aristotle, and Generally Have More Fun* (Harper, 2009). This particular blog entry offers tips for a quick mood makeover including "rid yourself of a nagging task" and just plain "act happy."

I Can Has Cheezburger? Network

icanhascheezburger.com

Browse the LOL cats, dogs, the Fail Blog ("laugh out loud" *schadenfreude*), or Engrishfunny.com here. You can also submit your own LOL photos and captions.

Engrish.com

engrish.com

Can't get enough mangled English? Visit this site for signs that read, "Don't jumping in the elevator," "Dumpling stuffed with the ovary and digestive organs of a crab," and "Dying right here is strictly prohibited."

YouTube: The Antwerp Train Station Gets a Treat!

www.youtube.com/watch?v=0UE3CNu_rtY

In this advertisement for a Belgian reality show, 200 dancers perform in the Antwerp Train Station to the "Do Re Mi" song from *The Sound of Music*. Dare you not to smile.

Geek Project: Laughing Baby

www.geekproject.com/william.aspx

When my friend Sandy is feeling blue, nothing cheers him faster than going onto YouTube to get his laughing baby fix. Back in 2005, Kjell-Ake Andersson took this video of his son William, who couldn't stop laughing when the microwave dinged. He keeps us giggling today!

The Onion

www.theonion.com

America's finest fake news source keeps us up-to-date with the exploits of the "area man" and the thoughts of six random subjects (who are always the same people). Sample headlines include "*New York Times* 'Faces of the Dead' Editor Just Needs a Couple More to Fill Out Corner" and "Work Friend Accidentally Becomes Real Friend." The Onion is available as a free iPhone app for comedy on the go (itunes.apple.com/us/app/the-onion/id363618575?mt=8).

Games

Moods manifest in the physical brain. According to the BBC Human Brain Map (www.bbc.co.uk/science/humanbody/body/

interactives/organs/brainmap), happiness is made up of three things: feeling physical pleasure, having a sense of purpose in life, and not feeling negative. That's right: "Your amygdala is responsible for generating negative emotions. To be happy, this part of your brain must be kept quiet."

This implies that a big part of being happy involves not being unhappy, that is, inhibiting activity in a deep, primitive part of the brain. "Working on non-emotional mental tasks inhibits the amygdala, which is why keeping yourself busy can cheer you up when you're feeling down."

Simple enough. Distract that pesky amygdala by playing these games.

Falling Sand Game

chir.ag/stuff/sand

Sand falls. You draw lines to manipulate it. More tools are available at the bottom of the page, including "plant" and "fire." Listen

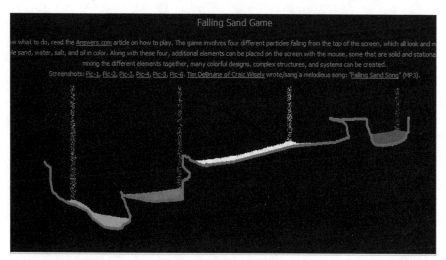

Falling Sand Game

to "The Falling Sand Song" (chir.ag/stuff/sand/falling_sand_by_ tim_debruine.mp3) while you play. Very Zen.

Yahoo! Games

games.yahoo.com

Here are arcade, board, and word games, most of them free with registration.

MSN Games Preview

games.msn.com

Visit MSN Games Preview to play free games like Solitaire and Bejeweled. Sign in with your Windows Live address (i.e., Hotmail) or share your scores with your pals on Facebook.

Shockwave.com Games

www.shockwave.com

Watch a short ad in exchange for playing a terrific assortment of Shockwave games for free.

Alive Games

www.alivegames.com

This site's free online games include Prime Suspects (a kind of Eye Spy—get your reading glasses out) and Big Kahuna Reef (think Bejeweled with scallops).

Pogo.com

www.pogo.com

Electronic Arts powers this game site, which is a favorite of my bridge-playing colleague Lora.

Sounds and Visions

I'm certain that a more serene environment could help calm our minds and help us to achieve our happiness goals. Here are some resources.

Pandora

www.pandora.com

Type the name of a song or an artist into the search box. Pandora will create an online radio station based on that artist or song and others like it for hours for free (with occasional commercial breaks.) Tim Westergren and his colleagues at Pandora's Music Genome Project did the librarian thing and categorized music based on its attributes: melody, harmony, instrumentation, and rhythm. The happy result is that users not only enjoy music that they know but get to explore new artists, too. The site charges a small fee for users who download more than 40 hours of music per month. Pandora has free apps for the iPhone (www.pandora.com/on-the-iphone) and Droid (in the Android Marketplace on your phone), finally making the phone (well, the smart phone) an effective music player!

Last.fm

www.last.fm

This service is owned by CBS and so has the deep pockets to host an incredible music catalog including classical and country music in addition to pop and hip hop. Get a free account and choose an artist or a song, and Last.fm will create a streaming station, building on your theme, using its "Audioscrobbler" technology. The site offers photos and background about the artist as the music plays. And wouldn't you know it, Last.fm has free apps for Android, BlackBerry, and iPhones (www.last.fm/hardware/apple).

Practice Meditation Online

www.musicdesi.com/soothing/online.html

While listening to soothing music, focus your mind by watching a candle flame flicker on your computer screen.

What Silver Lining?

Is the relentless drumbeat of cheerfulness in the face of loss and change driving you crazy? (Or, maybe, as Groucho Marx used to say, "That's not a drive, it's a short putt.") Perhaps these "Amygdala Rules, Frontal Cortex Drools" websites better suit your style.

Defensive Pessimism Quiz

www.wellesley.edu/Psychology/Norem/Quiz/quiz.html

Julie K. Norem, psychology professor at Wellesley College, has found that for some anxious people expecting and preparing for the worst makes them feel and perform better than trying to be optimistic. Is this your coping strategy? Find out by taking this short quiz.

California State University: Imposter Phenomenon

www.fullerton.edu/universityblues/self_steem/imposter_
phenomenon.htm

Some people feel a disconnect between their outward success and their inward state. They suffer from a distinct impression that they are living a lie and will soon be discovered for the imposters that they are. Read about imposter phenomenon in this article from the counseling center at the California State University at Fullerton.

KaliMunro.com: Clance IP Scale

www.kalimunro.com/self-quiz_imposter.html

Take this short self-test hosted by psychotherapist Kali Munro to see if you suffer from the imposter phenomenon.

Despair, Inc.

despair.com

If looking on the bright side has lost its luster, try this site. Find "de-motivational" posters with sayings like, "It Could Be That the

Purpose of Your Life Is Only to Serve as a Warning to Others." Buy "Bittersweets" Valentine candy (with sayings like "Table for 1" or "Cry on Q") and coffee mugs that are always "half empty."

Hope You're Happy

The web is filled with happy and fun ideas and activities. My only qualm is that they may keep us so content in our "neutral zone" that we will never want to move on to our new "beginnings."

Endnote

1. Sonja Lyubomirsky, Laura King, and Ed Diener, "The Benefits of Frequent Positive Affect: Does Happiness Lead to Success?" *Psychological Bulletin* 131, no. 6(2005): 803–855, www.apa.org/pubs/journals/releases/bul-1316803.pdf (accessed November 8, 2010).

Afterword

As I put the final touches on *The Internet Book of Life*, the web is not yet 20 years old. Yet, in just one generation, it has transformed the world and touched the lives of millions. It's a dynamic resource, yet I've found that many of the most useful websites go back to the early days. These are the type of stable resources I've tried to highlight in the book.

The Internet Book of Life is a travel guide of sorts, and as with any such reference, some of the resources it covers will change (or disappear) over time; many will be supplanted by even more wonderful resources. What will endure are our needs as human beings.

As long as the web exists, there will be sites that help us live more fully. While they will change over time, I'm going to do my best to update them—and add new sites of value—through my blog at imcdermott.wordpress.com.

If at any time the book and its supporting blog don't answer your most pressing questions, be sure to ask your local librarian for assistance.

That's what we are here for!

About the Author

Irene E. McDermott gains insight about the web from her daily frontline experience as reference librarian-slash-systems manager at the Crowell Public Library in San Marino, California. She writes about her discoveries in her column "Internet Express," which has appeared in *Searcher* magazine since 1997. She is the author of two editions of the book, *The Librarian's Internet Survival Guide: Strategies for the High-Tech Reference Desk* (2002, 2006, Information Today, Inc.). McDermott shares her Pasadena bungalow with her teenage son.

Index

H

Half.com, 99
Hamm, Trent, 112
Handy Guys Podcast, 119, *119*
Handyman Online, 125
Happiest Baby on the Block, The (Karp),
    63–64
happiness
    games, 268–270, *269*
    instant relief and mood enhancements,
        266–268
    overview, 261–266, 268–269
    pessimism, 272–273
    psychological tests, 263–264, *264*
    sound and vision resources, 270–271
    studies on, 264–266, *266*
Happiness Project, The, 267
Harding, John, 48
Harriet Buhai Center for Family Law, 49
Hartmann, Sarah, 37
Harvard Health Publications, 267
Hassett, Robin, 38
Hathaway, Sandee, 60–61
Hawaiian weddings, 42
Haynes, Craig, 214
Haynes Repair Manuals, 146
Hazelton, Ron, 117
H-C (Compulsive Hoarding Community),
    248
health and medicine. *See also* diet; fitness
    addiction recovery, 239–248, *241*, *245*,
        248, 249–250
    apps for, 223
    children and, 60, 61–69, *64*
    clinical trials, 224
    drugs, 223–224
    educational resources, 82
    exercise, 235–237
    food and health advice, 233–235, *234*

general information, 212–214, *213*, *215*
hospital discharge procedures, 222
lab testing and results interpretations,
    222–223
medical terminology and dictionaries,
    3, 222
mental, 220–221, 265
nonprofit organizations, 220
nutrition, 232–233
overview, 211–212
pet, 198–199
physician/dentist locator, 63, 221–222
site quality assessments, 225
specific conditions, 214–219, *219*
support groups, 249
symptom checkers, 212
teen information and advice, 99
Healthfinder.gov, 220
Health On the Net Foundation, 225
Healthy Children, 63
HealthyPet.com, 199
heart disease, 213, 215–216
Here Comes the Guide, 33
Hertz Car Sales, 148, *149*
HGTV (Home and Garden Television), 120
Hicks, Angie, 125–126
Hindu wedding traditions, 37
HippoCampus, 89
History.com, 83
history homework, 82–83
hoarding addictions, 248
Home Depot, 117
home improvement
    appliance repairs, 120–121
    apps for, 124
    contractors and professional services,
        125–126
    general resources, 116–120, *118*, *119*
    housekeeping and cleaning, 121–123,
        122

More Great Books from Information Today, Inc.

Point, Click, and Save
Mashup Mom's Guide to Saving and Making Money Online

By Rachel Singer Gordon

This immensely practical book and its supporting website provide clear tech-savvy advice to reassure readers who are new to the world of saving and earning money online, while providing an array of innovative ideas, strategies, and resources for those who have been clipping coupons (online *or* off) for years. Rachel Singer Gordon is "Mashup Mom"—a widely read blogger who combines high- and low-tech strategies to help her readers achieve financial objectives. Here, she helps money-conscious web users gain immediate relief from the pain of rising prices, find fabulous freebies, engage the whole family in the fun of using the web to create income, and much more!

304 pp/softbound/ISBN 978-0-910965-86-6 $19.95

Dancing With Digital Natives
Staying in Step With the Generation That's Transforming the Way Business Is Done

Edited by Michelle Manafy and Heidi Gautschi

Generational differences have always influenced how business is done, but in the case of digital natives—those immersed in digital technology from birth—we are witnessing a tectonic shift. As an always connected, socially networked generation increasingly dominates business and society, organizations can ignore the implications only at the risk of irrelevance. In this fascinating book, Michelle Manafy, Heidi Gautschi, and a stellar assemblage of experts from business and academia provide vital insights into the characteristics of this transformative generation. Here is an in-depth look at how digital natives work, shop, play, and learn, along with practical advice geared to help managers, marketers, coworkers, and educators maximize their interactions and create environments where everyone wins.

408 pp/hardbound/ISBN 978-0-910965-87-3 $27.95

Web of Deceit
Misinformation and Manipulation in the Age of Social Media

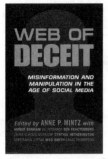

Edited by Anne P. Mintz

For all its amazing benefits, the worldwide social media phenomenon—epitomized by such sites and tools as Facebook, Myspace, eBay, Twitter, and Craigslist—has provided manipulative people and organizations with the tools (and human targets) that allow hoaxes and con games to be perpetrated on a vast scale. In this eye-opening follow-up to her popular 2002 book, *Web of Deception*, Anne P. Mintz brings together a team of expert researchers, journalists, and subject experts to explain how misinformation is intentionally spread and to illuminate the dangers in a range of critical areas. *Web of Deceit* is a must-read for any internet user who wants to avoid being victimized by liars, thieves, and propagandists in the age of ubiquitous social media.

December 2011/320 pp/softbound/ISBN 978-0-910965-91-0 $29.95

The Extreme Searcher's Internet Handbook, 3rd Edition
A Guide for the Serious Searcher

By Randolph Hock

The Extreme Searcher's Internet Handbook is the essential guide for anyone who uses the internet for research—librarians, teachers, students, writers, business professionals, and others who need to search the web proficiently. In this fully updated third edition, Ran Hock covers strategies and tools for all major areas of internet content. Readers with little to moderate searching experience will appreciate Hock's helpful, easy-to-follow advice, while experienced searchers will discover a wealth of new ideas, techniques, and resources.

368 pp/softbound/ISBN 978-0-910965-84-2 $24.95